ITALIAN/AMERICAN

ITALIAN/AMERICAN

IT'S A QCP COOKBOOK, BETCH!

GIANLUCA CONTE

Publisher Mike Sanders
Art & Design Director William Thomas
Editorial Director Ann Barton
Senior Editor Molly Ahuja
Assistant Director of Art & Design Rebecca Batchelor
Co-writer/Lifestyle Photographer Sophia Conte
Interior Photographer Matt Russell
Cover Photographer Stow Kelly
Recipe Developer/Food Stylist Bee Berrie
Food Styling Assisants Ryan Norton, Courtney Weise, and Meena Kumar
Prop Stylist Cate Kalus
Proofreader Claire Safran
Indexer Beverlee Day

First American Edition, 2024
Published in the United States by DK Publishing
1745 Broadway, 20th Floor, New York, NY 10019

The authorized representative in the EEA is Dorling Kindersley
Verlag GmbH. Arnulfstr. 124, 80636 Munich, Germany

Copyright @ 2024 by Gianluca Conte
DK, a Division of Penguin Random House LLC
23 24 25 26 27   10 9 8 7 6 5 4 3 2 1
001–337669–APR2024

A catalog record for this book
is available from the Library of Congress.
ISBN 978-0-7440-8839-7

DK books are available at special discounts when purchased
in bulk for sales promotions, premiums, fund-raising, or
educational use. For details, contact SpecialSales@dk.com

Printed and bound in China.

www.dk.com

This book was made with Forest
Stewardship Council™ certified
paper - one small step in DK's
commitment to a sustainable future.
**For more information go to
www.dk.com/our-green-pledge**

DEDICATION

To the most supportive parents imaginable:
I cannot thank you enough or express enough
appreciation. You both gave me your guidance
and wisdom to become the human I am today,
and I owe you all the world for it. Mom, you let
me kick you out of your kitchen when I filmed
videos in your home before I moved out, and you
always were ready to come back in when I
needed your help with a dish. Dad, you never
failed to call me if I cooked something wrong,
and I know you will forever send me new
delicious recipes to make. For this and many
more reasons, thank you and love you, Mamma
and Papa.

FAN DEDICATION

To anyone who has supported me and my content, I love and appreciate you more than you know. The support I have received has fueled me and will keep me going forever.

CONTENTS

INTRODUCTION

INTRODUCTION

Destiny is a real thing. I can't say I know my purpose in the world, but two things I do know are how to put on a show and how to make good food.

I made a name for myself on social media with my comedic, high-energy cooking videos, and became known for making pasta and saying "betch." Let me quickly explain how I got here, because I sure as hell did not expect to become a comedian, or a chef.

Not only is my father from Italy, but I am fortunate enough that he took my sisters and I to his hometown Ischia, a small island off the coast of Naples, every year when I was a child. Spending a month there every year during the summer gave me a real home away from home. It showed me how different life is in Europe and gave me the appreciation for culture and family.

Growing up, I wasn't an attention-seeker, but I did love to make people laugh and smile. Soon I began to realize I was pretty good at it. I began making music in high school and found another thing I was passionate about. After performing my music at my junior and senior proms, and feeling the energy from those singing along, I knew I wanted to spend the rest of my life entertaining. But I didn't know how or where to begin.

I went to college for a year and then realized I wasn't doing enough to pursue my true passions. My father offered to let me work for him at his incredible Italian restaurants in Charlotte, North Carolina, while I figured things out. I also took community college classes to study business—the idea being that I'd work alongside him and learn the restaurant business until he'd decide to let me take over the restaurants one day.

In August 2019, one of my closest friends, Stow, an incredible photographer who shot the cover of this cookbook, introduced me to TikTok. He said to me, "Bro, the girls will love you on here." I couldn't believe how easy it was to create and upload a video from my phone. My second day on the app, I walked into work after posting a video and realized... it was blowing up! I was gaining thousands of followers by the hour. I boasted to my coworkers, "It's over! I've done it! You don't understand!" I knew that once I got a platform, I would never stop giving people the content they wanted, and my work would exponentially grow. Around six months from then, toward the end of 2019, I had nearly 600,000 followers on TikTok—and I hadn't made a single cooking video. I was making funny, sporadic videos, and people loved my "anything goes" energy, but one video caused my whole path to take a turn.

"If *The Jersey Shore* Had a Cooking Show" was the title of my first cooking video. I didn't know how to cook much beyond the dish I made in the video. I sautéed some garlic and cherry tomatoes in olive oil, threw in some penne pasta and Parmesan cheese, and called it a dish. I wasn't too concerned about the recipe because my main focus was this over-the-top character with a heavy New Jersey/New York accent and unmatched energy. The engagement this video received encouraged me to create a second one, but with a twist. I turned this idea into its own series, *The Angry New Jersey Cooking Show*, in which I would act a little angrier in every episode I made. By my second episode, I had gone viral, with more than 30 million views on TikTok and millions across other platforms. People could not let go of these videos. They loved the character I played—and began to love the food I cooked! Every time I created a video, that was the first time I had ever made that dish, but no one knew! I guess you could say I'm a natural. Or you can say that I grew up with the most amazing Italian restaurants in Charlotte and have the best mentor ever, my dad.

Months later, I found myself filming only cooking content, and I wasn't mad about it. Making myself dinner for living? Hell yeah! I was still more focused on the comedy and entertainment of the video over the food I was preparing, but that soon changed.

One day my father called me, saying, "Gianluca, what are you doing? Why are you skipping steps? Please listen to me." I realized that maybe I should listen to the guy who grew up poor, immigrated to the United States, and worked his way from a busboy to one of the most successful entrepreneurs in Charlotte. The care that he puts into his work inspired me to do the same. From that moment on, I focused on making Italian dishes *right*. I can't say that I've fully mastered the cuisine, but with three years of experience of cooking pure Italian cuisine, I can confidently say I am on my way.

That "destiny" I mentioned earlier was my destiny to follow in my father's footsteps, without intending to. I started on my own path in life—leaving school, making music, and then creating videos to express myself—all to end up doing exactly what my father would do if he was in my shoes. He sacrificed everything he had to give me the life I have, and I have nothing but love and respect for that.

Follow your heart and the world will put you where you belong.

HOW TO USE THIS BOOK

Just like my videos, I wanted to keep this book very simple and easy to use. Most cookbooks include the exact amount of time to sauté, or the exact amount of salt or oil used in a dish. With my style of cooking, I encourage you to use your senses and eyeball it! I tend to say "a pinch of salt," or a "drizzle of olive oil," which doesn't have an exact amount. Don't stress it and just have fun!

Because the title of the book is *Italian/American*, I want to be sure you know which recipes are authentically Italian and which are not. On each recipe, I've indicated whether the dish is authentic Italian or American Italian (look for the flag tabs along the side of the pages). Also on each recipe, and elsewhere throughout the book, you will see a QR code. When you scan the QR code with your phone, you will be redirected to a link which will show you a video of either me pronouncing the name of the dish or another visual experience related to the information on the page. Finally, I've dedicated two sections to homemade pasta and homemade tomato sauce. Those two things are very important when we are talking about Italian food.

ESSENTIAL EQUIPMENT

Don't let the pretty kitchens and state of the art kitchen equipment fool you. Luxury is always nice, but by no means is it necessary. Certain tools, however, are absolutely necessary when making Italian food.

Dutch Oven: A Dutch oven is a large, cast iron pot that's great to use for slow cooking, searing food, making meat sauces, frying, and more. They can be pricey, but it's worth the investment for a better result.

Thin Tongs and Regular Tongs: Tongs are not just for picking things up and flipping them over. They can be used for so much more than that. I use tongs to sauté, to toss pasta, and for presentation purposes. Grab a ladle, scoop up some pasta with your tongs, twirl the pasta in the ladle, then set the ladle on a plate. Slide the ladle from under the tongs while squeezing the tongs. Slowly release. Then you will be left with the famous spaghetti twirl. Unless you screw it up.

Blender: Using a blender, smoothie bullet, emulsifier, or food processor is my preferred device for making pesto. Traditionally a mortar and pestle is used to crush the ingredients together, but ain't nobody got time for that.

Spider: This web-like tool, called a "spider," is my best friend in the kitchen. I barely ever need to use a colander because of this guy. It is like a mini, hand-held strainer, that you can use to grab pasta and then toss the pasta straight into the sauce. And no... it doesn't bite.

Knives: Having one solid, super-sharp chef's knife will save you so much time and energy when preparing vegetables. Don't play with knives like I do in my videos, because as we know, they are no joke. Having a variety of knives, to me, is optional. Invest in one good one, and take care of it like a baby.

Pots and Pans: Any type of pot or pan will get the job done, but investing in a high-end set can save you time and hassle when it comes to cooking and cleaning. Higher end pots and pans typically have heat-proof handles, are made with heavier materials, heat up quicker, and are sometimes oven and dishwasher safe (but do your research and check on that).

Grater: With the amount of cheese you will grate making the recipes from this book, it's important to have a durable cheese grater. I have broken a few grater handles from grating cheese too hard, but maybe that's just a me problem.

Bench Scraper: A bench scraper is a flat, metal tool that has so many uses in the kitchen. I use it for scooping my vegetables up from the cutting board and throwing them into the pan. I also use it while making homemade pasta to keep my hands clean while combining the ingredients before forming it into a dough. The best use, though, is for cleaning up your countertops, to scrape off any residue without causing damage.

Pasta Equipment: In my section dedicated to making homemade pasta (see page 72), I list all of the necessary tools and uses of each tool. This section is your homemade pasta "bible" and will leave you with no questions.

Wooden Kitchen Tools: The wooden spoon or spatula, also known as the Italian mother's primary weapon, may bring many some people PTSD... but hopefully it brings out more positive memories because of the delicious dishes made with it. I use it with almost every dish to stir sauces, sauté vegetables, and break up meat when making a meat sauce.

Mortar and Pestle: Using a mortar and pestle will level up your game in the kitchen when it comes to crushing black peppercorns or other whole dried spices and even chilies. The alternative to this traditional device is any type of blender, or for peppercorns, you could use a pepper grinder.

Food Mill: Using a food mill to crush your tomatoes when making homemade sauce will save you time and energy, and maximize the amount of juice extracted from the tomato. See page 11 for a more detailed description of how to use one of these guys.

Cutting Board: Wooden cutting boards are my preferred type of cutting board when it comes to prepping. They are durable and easy on your knives. They need to be taken care of, just like your knives, to get the most use out of them. Pro tip: If your cutting board is sliding while you cut, soak and ring out a sheet of paper towel (or a kitchen towel, if you want to be eco-friendly), then press it into the counter and place your cutting board over top to prevent it from moving.

Apron: WEAR AN APRON! Protect your skin and clothes. I might sound like a hypocrite because I don't wear a shirt under my apron, but it's your protection in the kitchen. Don't have one? Get yourself one of my signature "BETCH" aprons.

ESSENTIAL ITALIAN INGREDIENTS

Italian cuisine is simple. With simplicity, the quality and freshness of your ingredients makes or breaks your dish. Listed below are some of the most commonly used ingredients in Italian cooking. If you plan to make even a few of the dishes from the book, get your cabinets stocked, betch.

Extra-Virgin Olive Oil: Also known as "evoo," extra-virgin olive oil is considered the best grade of olive oil. It is recognized for its high quality and bold flavor. If it's not good enough to drink, you may need to reconsider your purchase.

Garlic: In southern Italy, garlic is typically used as an ingredient to enhance flavor. I am a garlic lover, so in this cookbook, you will learn the various ways I prepare and cook with garlic. For example, when sautéing garlic, I sometimes lightly crush the cloves before adding them to the pan and then discard them (or eat them) once the flavor has been infused to give the dish a subtle garlic flavor. Or I slice or mince the cloves before sautéing them for a stronger flavor.

Red Pepper Flakes and Calabrian Chiles: Also known as crushed red pepper flakes, this spice adds moderate heat to tomato sauces, pastas, and pizzas. Using real calabrian chiles, typically found in a jar with oil, adds a very bold spice to the dish. The flavor outweighs the spice, although it's got a good kick.

Salt and Black Pepper: "A little salt in there, and some black peppa." If you've seen my videos, you've probably heard me say that a few hundred times. Most dishes require salt and pepper to enhance or add flavor. Grinding peppercorns in a pepper grinder, or by hand using a mortar and pestle, makes an unexpected difference of flavor. Store bought pre-ground pepper doesn't cut it for me. Cooking with kosher salt is ideal, and finishing the dish with a light sprinkle of flaky salt is also great. I honestly use flaky salt for everything, not for any specific reason. I just like it.

Fresh Herbs: In Italian cuisine, basil and parsley are the two most commonly used herbs. Basil is, hands down, my favorite herb. It's the foundation of pesto and it's super easy to grow. Parsley is often used as a garnish but also is added to pastas. I always recommend fresh herbs in my recipes. There is never an instance where I will use dried parsley and basil, it's nowhere comparable to fresh. Dried oregano is the only dried Italian herb I commonly use.

Pasta: Pasta, BETCH! In most dishes you can use your preferred choice of pasta, but a few recipes work better with certain shapes of pasta. For most seafood pastas, for example, it's best to use linguine or spaghetti. For sauce-heavy pastas, fusilli is one of my favorite shapes because of its ability to hold the sauce within its ridges. Ultimately, it's up to you to experiment with the pasta shapes. Fresh pasta is always an upgrade to a dish. If you wish to level up, you can refer to my fresh pasta section (see page 72), where I show you how to make many different shapes.

Cheese: Hard cheeses such as Parmigiano-Reggiano and Pecorino Romano are the most commonly used cheeses in Italian cooking. Parmigiano Reggiano is typically aged from two to three years and holds one of the most bold but delicious flavors of all cheeses, in my opinion. Pecorino cheese is made from sheep's milk and is very salty. Mozzarella is a soft cheese used for melting in dishes, like lasagna, baked pasta, and pizza. Each cheese compliments the dishes in their own way, but don't hesitate to try different cheeses if you want to experiment.

Wine: For most fish dishes that call for wine, you can use any dry white, like Pinot Grigio or Sauvignon Blanc. For red wine used in a meat sauce, it's best to use a Cabernet Sauvignon, Pinot Noir, or Merlot. Marsala wine has a very nutty, rich flavor, making it such a popular cooking wine. The sauce it creates is so specific in flavor that most dishes it's used in have the name "Marsala" in it.

Tomatoes: Tomatoes are so commonly used through this cookbook that I have made a section dedicated to each use of different tomatoes. Fresh sauce always wins, but jarred and canned tomatoes have their uses as well.

Flour: Using 00 flour for your breading and homemade pasta will make a magical difference. 00 flour is a finely sifted italian flour, commonly used for making Neapolitan pizza, but is used as the Italian all-purpose flour. Order some online or source it from an Italian market (some grocery stores carry it), but if you use all-purpose flour, it's no problem.

Eggs: Eggs have a few uses throughout the book. One dish, carbonara, uses eggs as the main ingredient. Homemade pasta will also require eggs. Lastly, any time you are breading meat, like a chicken Parmesan, you will use eggs to bind the bread crumbs to the meat.

Bread Crumbs: I've never been the one to make fresh bread crumbs, but it's important to get an Italian brand of bread crumbs and use them up before they go stale. A stale breading will ruin your dish.

ANTIPASTI

PROSCIUTTO E MELONE
(PROSCIUTTO AND MELON)

"pro-shoot-oh eh meh-lone-eh"

SERVES: 6–8
PREP: 10 minutes
COOK: None

Pork and fruit? Don't be scared. This combination of sweet and salty is so easy to make, requires no cooking, and makes a great summer snack.

1 ripe cantaloupe melon

5 ounces (140g) prosciutto crudo, thinly sliced

8 ounces (225g) small fresh mozzarella balls or pearls

2 tablespoons balsamic fig glaze

1 small bunch of mint, leaves picked off, for garnish

1 Cut the cantaloupe in half. Scoop out the seeds with a spoon and discard them. Cut each cantaloupe half into 8 wedges and then remove and discard the rind from each wedge.

2 Wrap 1 slice of prosciutto tightly around each wedge and place on a serving plate.

3 Scatter the drained mozzarella balls around the plate.

4 Lightly drizzle some balsamic fig glaze over the plate, garnish with mint, and serve.

BUON APPETITO, BETCH!

ALICI MARINATE
(MARINATED ANCHOVIES)

"a-lee-chee ma-ree-na-teh"

SERVES: 4
PREP: 30 minutes (plus 6 hours or overnight to marinate)
COOK: None

A typical dish from all over southern Italy, alici marinate is a simple taste of the ocean. This was a must-have appetizer for my family whenever we would enjoy lunch by the sea on the coast of Italy. The ingredients are simple, but the freshness of the anchovies is vital to the flavor.

1 pound (450g) fresh whole anchovies

1 cup white vinegar

1 cup extra virgin olive oil

1 tablespoon dried oregano

¼ teaspoon chopped peperoncino chili or red chili flakes

2 tablespoons chopped Italian flat-leaf parsley

2 garlic cloves, sliced paper thin

1 teaspoon flaky salt

1 lemon wedge, for garnish

1 Using scissors, cut off the fins of the anchovies. Using a sharp paring knife, carefully slit each fish along the belly, head to tail, but do not cut through it. Remove the insides using a teaspoon or your thumb, and discard.

2 Cut off the head with a paring knife or scissors, and carefully pull out the spine and other larger bones with your fingertips or tweezers.

3 Separate the two little filets and then rinse them well with plenty of cold water. Repeat with the remaining anchovies.

4 Arrange a layer of the anchovies, skin-side down, in a small glass or ceramic dish (approximately 8x10 inch [20x20 cm]), and lightly drizzle some of the white vinegar over the top. Keep layering and drizzling the vinegar until you've used all of the filets.

5 Cover and marinate in the refrigerator for at least 4 hours or overnight.

6 After the anchovies have marinated, rinse them and pat them dry with paper towels. Clean out the dish.

7 Arrange a layer of anchovies in the clean dish and drizzle extra virgin olive oil over the top. Sprinkle the fish with some of the oregano, peperoncino chili, Italian flat-leaf parsley, garlic, and a pinch of salt. Repeat with another layer of anchovies and seasonings until you've used all the anchovies.

8 Cover and marinate in the refrigerator for at least 2 hours.

9 Remove from the refrigerator, and let rest for 30 minutes at room temperature before removing the anchovies. Arrange on a dish with a squeeze of fresh lemon juice and serve.

BUON APPETITO, BETCH!

INSALATA DI FAGIOLI
(TUSCAN BEAN SALAD)

"een-sah-lah-tah dee fah-jio-lee"

SERVES: 4
PREP: 15 minutes (plus 2 hours over overnight to marinate)
COOK: None

This bean salad is famous at my father's restaurants in Charlotte, NC. Marinated in imported Italian extra virgin olive oil and served on top of freshly baked crusty Italian bread, what's not to love? People and restaurants have tried to recreate it for years but this is the real recipe.

1 × 15-ounce (425g) can cannellini beans

2 Roma tomatoes

¼ red onion, very finely diced

1 garlic clove, minced

½ small bunch of basil, leaves picked off and chopped

¼ small bunch of Italian flat-leaf parsley, leaves picked off and chopped

½ teaspoon chopped peperoncino or red chili flakes

¼ cup extra virgin olive oil

1 large pinch of flaky sea salt

Freshly ground black pepper

Fresh Italian bread, for serving

1 Drain the cannellini beans and rinse under cold water.

2 Prepare the Roma tomatoes by cutting down the "cheeks" lengthwise, scooping out the seeds, and dicing the flesh. Discard the seeds and the stalk.

3 In a medium bowl, combine the beans, tomatoes, red onion, garlic, basil, Italian flat-leaf parsley, peperoncino or red chili flakes, extra virgin olive oil, salt, and pepper until all the ingredients are evenly distributed.

4 Transfer to an airtight container and set in the refrigerator to marinate for at least 2 hours or up to overnight.

5 Serve at room temperature with fresh Italian bread. Drain any excess oil if needed before serving.

BUON APPETITO, BETCH!

BEEF CARPACCIO

"car-pach-io"

SERVES: 4
PREP: 2 hours
COOK: None

Carpaccio is raw meat, so eat at your own risk. This is a delicacy for a reason, and it's best served on a bed of fresh arugula or my Insalata Tricolore (page 200).

8–10 ounces (225–285g) beef tenderloin

1 cup baby arugula leaves

1 small fennel bulb, finely sliced

1 small head radicchio, finely sliced

1 drizzle of extra virgin olive oil

1 pinch of flaky sea salt

1 lemon, halved

1 drizzle of truffle oil (optional)

¼ cup freshly shaved Parmesan cheese, for garnish

Freshly ground black pepper

1. Wrap the beef tenderloin in butcher's paper or plastic wrap. Place in the refrigerator overnight to chill until firm or in the freezer for 2 hours.

2. Using a large sharp knife, carefully slice the meat into the thinnest slices possible.

3. Place each slice onto a clean cutting board, and gently pound the meat with the heel of your hand to thin it out a little more. Carefully transfer the slice to a large plate, and repeat with the remaining meat.

4. In a large salad bowl, combine the arugula, fennel, and radicchio.

5. Add the extra virgin olive oil, salt, and juice from ½ of the lemon to the salad. Mix well to dress.

6. Spread the salad on a serving plate and add the sliced beef on top.

7. Drizzle the remaining ½ lemon juice over the meat, along with the truffle oil (if using). Garnish with some Parmesan cheese curls, season with salt and pepper, and serve immediately.

BUON APPETITO, BETCH!

CAESAR SALAD

SERVES: 4
PREP: 5 minutes
COOK: 15 minutes

This isn't pasta, but it is the most popular and classic salad on the menu almost anywhere you go, including most Italian restaurants. If I'm going to eat a Caesar salad, I want the best one in the world. So here you go: the best Caesar salad recipe in the world.

FOR THE CROUTONS:

1 loaf French or sourdough bread

2–3 tablespoons extra virgin olive oil

2 large pinches of flaky sea salt

2 large pinches of freshly ground black pepper

½ cup freshly grated Parmesan cheese

FOR THE DRESSING:

½ 2-ounce (55g) can preserved anchovy fillets packed in oil (about 6)

2 garlic cloves

1 large egg yolk

4 tablespoons fresh lemon juice

¼ teaspoon freshly ground black pepper

1 teaspoon Dijon mustard

1 cup neutral oil, such as grapeseed

¼ cup freshly grated Parmesan cheese

FOR THE SALAD:

2 large heads romaine lettuce, washed and chopped into ½-inch (1.25cm) slices

Freshly shaved Parmesan cheese

Freshly ground black pepper

FOR THE CROUTONS:

1 Preheat the oven to 375°F (190°C).

2 Cut the French or sourdough bread in half lengthwise and then cut into ¾-inch (2cm) cubes.

3 In a large bowl, toss the bread cubes with the extra virgin olive oil, salt, pepper, and Parmesan cheese.

4 Spread the croutons in an even layer on a baking sheet, and bake for 12 to 15 minutes or until golden, turning the croutons halfway through the cook time to ensure they toast evenly.

5 Remove from the oven and allow to cool.

FOR THE DRESSING:

1 Mince the anchovies and garlic and combine into a fine paste using the side of the knife. Set aside.

2 In a medium bowl, whisk together the egg yolk, lemon juice, pepper, and Dijon mustard.

3 Slowly whisk in the oil, one spoonful at a time.

4 Add in the anchovy and garlic paste, Parmesan, and a splash of water if necessary to thin the dressing, and stir to combine.

FOR THE SALAD:

1 In a large bowl, add the romaine. Pour about ¾ cup dressing over the romaine and toss to coat using tongs. Taste, and add more dressing if needed.

2 Place the dressed romaine in a serving bowl, top with croutons, and generously add some shaved Parmesan. Grind some pepper on top to finish, and serve.

TIP *If there is any dressing left over, store it in an airtight container in the fridge for up to 3 days.*

BUON APPETITO, BETCH!

CAPRESE PASTA SALAD

"cah-preh-zseh"

SERVES: 4
PREP: 15 minutes
COOK: 10 minutes

I'm a sucker for pasta, as you might guess, so I had no choice but to turn this classic salad into a pasta salad. Everything's better with pasta—even ice cream! (I'm kidding.) This healthy and refreshing pasta salad is best in the summer when the produce is fresh and you're feeling the best.

12 ounces (340g) farfalle pasta

4 tablespoons extra virgin olive oil

1 pinch of flaky sea salt

Freshly ground black pepper

1 garlic clove, puréed

8 ounces (225g) small fresh mozzarella balls or pearls

1½ cups cherry tomatoes, halved

½ bunch of basil, leaves picked off and finely sliced

1 Bring a large pot of salted water to a boil over high heat. Add the farfalle pasta and cook per the package instructions until just al dente. Drain the farfalle, and set aside to cool in a large bowl.

2 In a small bowl, whisk together the extra virgin olive oil, salt, pepper, and garlic. Drizzle over the farfalle.

3 Add the drained mozzarella balls, cherry tomatoes, and basil to the farfalle. Mix well.

4 Season with more salt and pepper to taste, and serve immediately.

TIP *Be sure to pick the freshest-looking basil because it serves as your greens in this salad. Any leftovers can be stored in an airtight container in the refrigerator for up to 3 days.*

BUON APPETITO, BETCH!

PANZANELLA CON BURRATA
(BURRATA PANZANELLA SALAD)
"pan-zah-nell-ah cone boo-rah-tah"

SERVES: 4
PREP: 20 minutes (plus marinating time)
COOK: 12 minutes

This Tuscan salad is a great way to use up any bread that is a day or two old. The bread needs to be the hearty artisan kind with a crunchy crust, like ciabatta, Tuscan, or sourdough. Bursting with ripe tomatoes, this refreshing dish is best enjoyed in the summertime while the tomatoes are in peak season. Light, fresh, and full of flavor, especially when paired with fresh burrata.

½ loaf Italian bread or 2 ciabatta rolls, stale preferred

2 tablespoons extra virgin olive oil

Flaky sea salt and freshly ground black pepper

1 small red onion, very thinly sliced into half moons

1 tablespoon red wine vinegar

1 large garlic clove, minced

2 cups mixed-color cherry and heirloom tomatoes

¾ teaspoon dried oregano, to taste

½ small bunch of basil, leaves picked off and finely chopped

1 handful of arugula leaves

1 tablespoon fresh lemon juice

1 medium ball burrata, about 8 ounces (220g)

1 If you are not using stale bread, allow the Italian bread or ciabatta to sit out overnight to dry.

2 Preheat the oven to 400°F (200°C).

3 Tear or chop the bread into large bite-sized pieces and then arrange them in a single layer on a baking sheet. Drizzle with extra virgin olive oil, season with salt and pepper, and bake for 10 to 12 minutes or until the edges appear crispy but the inside is chewy. Remove from the oven and allow the bread to cool for a few minutes on the baking sheet.

4 In a medium bowl, combine the red onion, red wine vinegar, and garlic. Set aside to soften until you're ready to combine it with the tomatoes.

5 Chop the cherry and heirloom tomatoes and add them to a large bowl. Add the oregano, basil, arugula, and bread chunks, and mix well. Add the onion mixture and its liquid and the lemon juice and stir. The stale bread will absorb all the delicious juices.

6 Remove the burrata from its liquid and gently pat dry with paper towels. Tear the burrata into large bite-sized pieces and arrange over the top of the salad. Season and serve.

TIP *You can serve this salad immediately, or you can let it sit for 30 minutes or up to 2 hours at room temperature. The longer you allow the salad to sit, the more the flavor develops! That said, this is not a salad that does well as leftovers. Drizzle a little more olive oil over the top if needed before serving.*

BUON APPETITO, BETCH!

BRUSCHETTA

"broo-skett-ah"

SERVES: 4
PREP: 10 minutes
COOK: 10 minutes

In Italian, *bruschetta* is pronounced *broo-skett-ah.* I learned this the hard way, as I've had millions of Italians across the internet judge my pronunciation. Do your best, and try to impress with the correct pronunciation. You can find this classic appetizer in almost every Italian restaurant around the world. My father and I like to use cherry tomatoes to bring this recipe to life because they're bursting with flavor and have a lower water content, which helps keep the bread from getting soggy.

11 ounces (320g) cherry tomatoes, quartered

1 pinch of flaky sea salt

Freshly ground black pepper

3 tablespoons extra virgin olive oil

½ small bunch of basil, leaves picked off and finely chopped

4 large slices Italian bread (ciabatta) or sourdough, about ½-inch (2.5cm) thick

2 garlic cloves, peeled and lightly crushed

1 In a medium bowl, combine the cherry tomatoes, salt, pepper, 1 tablespoon of the extra virgin olive oil, and the basil.

2 Set the bowl aside to marinate for at least 5 minutes. The longer you wait, the better it tastes. (My mom always told me, "Patience is a virtue," but when it comes to delicious bruschetta, I can't wait for long!)

3 Lightly brush each side of the Italian bread with the remaining 2 tablespoons of olive oil.

4 On a grill preheated to medium or in a cast-iron skillet over medium heat, toast the bread for 1–2 minutes per side, or until both sides are golden brown and lightly charred. Transfer to a serving plate and allow to cool for a few minutes.

5 Rub each slice of bread with a clove of garlic. (The rough texture of the toasted bread will collect some of the delicious garlic—you'll love it!) Switch to the second clove when the first one looks like it's ready to fall apart.

6 Spoon a generous amount of the tomato mixture on top of each bread slice. Season with more salt and pepper and serve immediately.

TIP *Bruschetta is best eaten fresh, but you can prepare the tomato mixture ahead and store it in an airtight container in the refrigerator for up to 2 days. Also, any variety of ripe tomatoes will work in place of the cherries.*

BUON APPETITO, BETCH!

CAPONATA
WITH CROSTINI

"kah-poh-nah-tah"

SERVES: 4 people
PREP: 40 minutes
COOK: 40 minutes

Caponata is a traditional Sicilian dish with an aromatic sweet and sour flavor. It can be served at any temperature but my preference is room temp! Serve with crusty bread or on top of crostini.

FOR THE EGGPLANT:
2 medium eggplants
1 teaspoon flaky sea salt
3–4 tablespoons extra virgin olive oil, plus more for serving
¼ cup pine nuts
1 medium white onion, diced
½ cup diced celery
1 tablespoon capers, drained
½ cup green Italian olives, pitted and diced
2 cups canned chopped tomatoes
2 tablespoons tomato purée
¼ cup white wine vinegar
¼ cup sugar
Freshly ground black pepper
¼ small bunch of basil, finely chopped, for garnish

FOR THE CROSTINI:
1 Italian baguette or ciabatta, sliced into rounds
2 tablespoons olive oil
Flaky sea salt

1 Wash the eggplants and pat dry with a paper towel. Cut each eggplant into cubes ½ inch (1.25cm) thick, place in a colander in the sink, and generously sprinkle with salt. Stir to coat and let sit for 30 minutes to reduce the bitterness. Pat dry before cooking.

2 Preheat the oven 350°F (180°C).

3 Place the eggplant cubes in a single layer on a baking sheet, drizzle evenly with 2 tablespoons of the olive oil, and roast for 25 to 30 minutes or until the edges are a little golden. Remove from the oven and set aside.

4 About 5 minutes before the eggplant is finished cooking, prepare the crostini. Arrange the Italian baguette or ciabatta slices in a single layer on another baking sheet and brush each side with a little olive oil. Place in the hot oven for 3 to 5 minutes or until toasted. Remove from the oven and set aside.

5 In a small frying pan over medium heat, toast the pine nuts until light brown. Be sure to keep an eye on the pine nuts because they can burn quickly. Remove from the heat and set aside in a bowl.

6 In a large pan over medium heat, pour in the remaining olive oil. When the oil is hot, add the white onion, and cook until softened and lightly golden. Add the celery and cook for a few more minutes until the celery has softened. Add the capers, green Italian olives, toasted pine nuts, and chopped tomatoes, and stir to mix. Reduce the heat to low, cover, and cook for 10 minutes.

7 In a small bowl, mix together the tomato purée, white vinegar, and sugar. (This makes an Italian version of a sweet-and-sour sauce).

8 Pour the sauce into the pan. Increase the heat to medium-low and cook for 5 minutes to reduce the vinegar smell. Add the roasted eggplant and cook, stirring, for 1 or 2 minutes.

9 Arrange the crostini slices on a large board or platter and evenly divide the eggplant mixture among the slices. Season with salt and pepper, drizzle a little extra virgin olive oil on top, garnish with some fresh basil, and serve.

BUON APPETITO, BETCH!

TRUFFLED GARLIC BREAD

SERVES: 6
PREP: 5 minutes
COOK: 45 minutes

"Garlic bread isn't Italian? But they serve it at Olive Garden!" You will not find garlic bread in most of Italy, but there's no denying its amazing flavor. What is already a simple and delish side dish gets elevated here with the truffle. The result is something magical.

2 whole garlic heads, skin on

2 tablespoons extra virgin olive oil

4 ounces (115g) unsalted butter, softened

1 fresh black truffle, shaved, or 2 teaspoons truffle oil

1 pinch of flaky truffle salt

Freshly ground black pepper

½ bunch of Italian flat-leaf parsley, leaves picked off and finely chopped

1 loaf ciabatta or French bread, cut lengthwise

2 tablespoons freshly grated Parmesan cheese (optional)

SPECIAL EQUIPMENT
Food processor

1. Preheat the oven to 425°F (220°C). Line a baking sheet with a piece of foil large enough to wrap both heads of garlic in.

2. Slice the garlic heads in half horizontally, and place them on the foil. Drizzle the exposed garlic cloves with a generous amount of extra virgin olive oil, and lightly brush or rub it into the cloves. Loosely seal the foil around the garlic.

3. Roast the garlic for about 30 minutes or until it's golden and soft to touch.

4. Remove the garlic from the oven, and allow it to cool a little. Unwrap from the foil and then squeeze the cloves out of the bulb and either into a food processor or onto a cutting board. Add the butter, shaved black truffle or truffle oil, truffle salt, pepper, and 1 tablespoon Italian flat-leaf parsley. Blend until combined if using the food processor; if chopping, crush the soft cloves with the back of your knife and purée them by chopping them finely with the other ingredients.

5. Place the ciabatta or French bread on the baking sheet and slice in half lengthwise. Using a butter knife or a pastry brush, thoroughly coat the cut surface of the bread with the truffled garlic butter.

6. Bake for 10 to 15 minutes or until slightly golden. During the last 2 minutes of the cook time, top with the Parmesan cheese (if using).

7. Garnish with the remaining parsley and serve hot.

BUON APPETITO, BETCH!

CARCIOFI ALLA ROMANA
(ROMAN BRAISED ARTICHOKES)

"car-chio-fee a-la ro-ma-na"

SERVES: 4
PREP: 20 minutes
COOK: 60 minutes

You can't say you don't like artichokes until you try them the Italian way. Roman-style artichokes is a traditional dish made with Romanesco artichokes, which are round and purple and have thornless leaves, making them entirely edible. This dish can be served as an appetizer or a side dish and is best enjoyed during the spring, when artichokes are in season.

TO PREPARE THE ARTICHOKES:

2 medium lemons

4 medium Romanesco artichokes, about 12 ounces (340g) each

2 tablespoons olive oil

¼ cup chopped Italian flat-leaf parsley

2 tablespoons chopped mint leaves

2 tablespoons chopped oregano leaves

2 garlic cloves, finely minced

1 pinch of flaky sea salt

Freshly ground black pepper

TO COOK THE ARTICHOKES:

1 cup extra virgin olive oil, plus more for drizzling

1 pinch of flaky sea salt

Freshly ground black pepper

1 Cut 1 lemon in half, and squeeze the juice into a large bowl half full of cold water. Rub the remaining part of the lemon on your hands to prevent them from blackening while you clean the artichokes.

2 Cut off the stem of each Romanesco artichoke at the base where the leaves form the bottom of the bulb. Start removing the outer leaves by hand, snapping each one down and off until you get to the softer heart leaves. Try to remove about two thirds to three fourths of the outer leaves. Using your fingers, open and spread apart the inner heart leaves. Using a small spoon, scrape out the hairy choke in the center of each heart.

3 Add the cleaned artichokes to the bowl of lemon water. Press a paper towel or clean kitchen towel into the water over the artichokes to keep them submerged, and set aside to soak until you're ready to start steaming.

4 In a small bowl, mix together the olive oil, Italian flat-leaf parsley, mint, oregano, and garlic. Season with salt and pepper.

5 Remove the artichokes from the lemon water and rub each artichoke with the herb mixture. Be sure to get the herb mixture into every crevice.

6 Add the extra virgin olive oil and 1 cup of water to a pot just large enough to hold all the artichokes side by side so they can lay flat with their stems pointing up.

7 Place the artichokes in the pot and season them with salt and pepper.

8 Set the pot over medium-high heat and bring to a boil. Reduce the heat to low, cover, and simmer for about 45 to 60 minutes or until the artichokes are tender.

9 Remove the last couple of outside leaves if they are discolored. Serve with a drizzle of olive oil and the remaining lemon, cut into wedges.

TIP *When cleaning artichokes, it's best to wear gloves or rub your hands with lemon juice because artichokes have a high amount of antioxidants and react with oxygen. Lemon juice slows down the oxidation which will prevent the artichokes and your hands from turning brown.*

BUON APPETITO, BETCH!

FRITTATA DI ZUCCHINE
(ZUCCHINI FRITTATA)

"free-tah-tah dee zoo-keen-eh"

SERVES: 4
PREP: 10 minutes
COOK: 20 minutes

Nothing beats the smell of frittata in the morning. Frittata is the Italian version of an omelette except it is flat, moist, and not folded. Growing up my mom would always use up whatever vegetables she had on hand and throw together the BEST frittata. Best enjoyed for brunch but can also be eaten as a light dinner.

1–2 tablespoons extra virgin olive oil

1½ shallots, finely sliced

2 medium zucchini, cut into thin rounds

6 eggs

1 large pinch of flaky sea salt

Freshly ground black pepper

2 tablespoons chopped Italian flat-leaf parsley

½ cup finely grated Parmesan cheese

1 In a small (6-inch/15cm) frying pan over medium heat, warm the olive oil. When the oil is hot, add the shallots and sauté for 1 minute over low heat.

2 Add the zucchini rounds and sauté for 8 to 10 minutes, or until the zucchini is cooked and the edges have a little color.

3 Into a medium bowl, crack the eggs. Season with salt and pepper, add 1 tablespoon Italian flat-leaf parsley, and lightly whisk with a fork.

4 Pour the eggs into the pan, but *do not stir*. Reduce the heat to medium-low.

5 Sprinkle the Parmesan cheese over the eggs, cover the pan, and cook for 10 to 12 minutes. Some small bubbles and steam will escape as the eggs cook, so be careful not to let the bottom burn; reduce the heat to low if necessary. The frittata is cooked when the eggs have set on the bottom. There should be no uncooked egg visible.

6 Using a spatula, gently loosen the frittata edges from the sides of the pan, and carefully slide it from the pan onto a plate or board.

7 Garnish with the remaining 1 tablespoon parsley and serve.

BUON APPETITO, BETCH!

FIORI DI ZUCCA
(ZUCCHINI FLOWER)

"fee-ore-ee dee zoo-kah"

SERVES: 4
PREP: 5 minutes
COOK: 5 minutes

My FAVORITE Italian street snack—fried zucchini flowers. Fluffy, savory, and simply perfect.

8–12 fresh zucchini flowers

¾ cup type 00 or all-purpose flour

1 tablespoon semolina flour

1 small pinch of saffron threads (optional)

1 cup cold sparkling water

1 pinch of flaky sea salt

1 cup vegetable oil, for frying

1 lemon, cut into wedges, for serving

1   Wash the zucchini flowers well under cold running water, but don't let them soak. Gently pat them dry with a paper towel or cloth.

2   Remove and discard the green inner parts of the flower using the tip of a pair of scissors or tweezers. Keep the stem intact, but trim it to about ½ inch (1.25cm) long.

3   In a medium bowl, pour the cold sparkling water.

4   Add in the all-purpose flour, a ¼ of a cup at a time. Then add in the semolina flour, salt, and saffron (if using) until you have the consistency of pancake batter.

5   In a medium frying pan over medium-high heat, warm the vegetable oil until very hot. To test to see if it's ready, add a droplet of batter to the pan. If it sizzles, it's ready.

6   Line a large plate with paper towels.

7   Pinching the top of the flowers closed with your fingers so no batter gets inside, dip the flowers in the batter to coat the outside.

8   Gently add the flowers to the hot oil, turning it down a bit if it spits too violently, and fry for 1 or 2 minutes. Turn over the flowers and fry for 1 or 2 minutes more or until they're golden all over.

9   Carefully remove the fried flowers from the oil and transfer them to the paper towel–lined plate to drain.

10 Serve hot with a squeeze of fresh lemon juice.

BUON APPETITO, BETCH!

CROCCHETTE DI PATATE
(POTATO CROQUETTES)

"crow-keh-teh dee pah-tah-teh"

SERVES: 4 (about 20 croquettes)
PREP: 30 minutes
COOK: 35 minutes

F%$K A MOZZARELLA STICK! These potato croquettes are a true street snack. These are best enjoyed while wandering the streets of Naples. But of course, also enjoy them at home as an appetizer.

2 pounds (1kg) small or medium red potatoes, skin on

1 medium ball fresh mozzarella, about 5 ounces (140g)

5–6 slices ham, about 5 ounces (140g)

2 egg yolks

¾ cup grated Parmigiano-Reggiano cheese

Flaky sea salt and freshly ground black pepper

¼ teaspoon ground nutmeg, or to taste

1 cup freshly grated Pecorino Romano or Parmesan cheese

1 small bunch of Italian flat-leaf parsley, leaves picked off and chopped

2 eggs

7 ounces (200g) bread crumbs

2 cups olive oil, for frying

SPECIAL EQUIPMENT

Potato ricer or masher

1 Scrub the red potatoes under running water to remove any dirt.

2 Bring a large pot of salted water to boil over medium-high heat. Add the whole, skin-on potatoes and cook for 20 to 30 minutes or until fork-tender.

3 Cut the mozzarella and ham into small cubes, combine them in a medium bowl, and set aside.

4 Drain the potatoes and let them cool a little until they're easy to handle. Using the tip of a spoon, lift and peel away the skin, keeping as much of the waxy potato as possible. Place the peeled potatoes in a large bowl.

5 While the potatoes are still warm, use a potato ricer or a fork to mash them into a smooth consistency—no lumps.

6 In a small bowl, combine the egg yolks, Parmigiano-Reggiano cheese, salt, pepper, and nutmeg. Add to the mashed potatoes and mix well.

7 Add the Pecorino Romano cheese and Italian flat-leaf parsley to the potato mixture. Using your hand, mix well. The mash should start to come together easily.

8 Line a baking sheet with parchment paper. Line a plate with paper towels.

9 Wet your hands, scoop a golf ball–size portion of the potato mixture, and flatten it into a rough disc shape in your palm.

10 Spoon about 1 teaspoon of the mozzarella and ham mixture into the center of the disc, and use your fingers to press and close the potato mixture all around the filling. Roll the croquette into a cylinder shape, and gently press both ends to ensure no filling escapes. Place the croquette on the prepared baking sheet, and repeat with the remaining potato and filling mixtures.

11 In a shallow bowl, beat the 2 whole eggs. In another shallow bowl, place the bread crumbs. Coat each croquette in the beaten eggs first and then in the bread crumbs. Return them to the baking sheet.

12 In a medium frying pan over medium-high heat, heat about 1 inch (2.5cm) of olive oil. When the oil is hot, add a few croquettes at a time, being careful to avoid the spitting oil. Cook for five minutes, turning them every few minutes with tongs until they are evenly browned all over.

13 Using a slotted spoon or tongs, transfer the croquettes from the oil to the paper towel–lined plate to drain. Repeat with the remaining croquettes. Serve hot.

BUON APPETITO, BETCH!

PARMIGIANA DI MELANZANE
(EGGPLANT PARMESEAN)

(par-me-g-ana dee mel-aan-zah-neh)

SERVES: 4–6
PREP: 30 minutes
COOK: 1 hour

Ah... The lasagna of vegetables. Eggplant parmesan is hands down one of the most classic dishes in Italian cuisine, and for a reason of course. The fried eggplant and cheeses become best friends to make this a mouth-watering appetizer.

TO PREPARE THE EGGPLANT:

2 medium eggplants

A few pinches of table salt

FOR THE SAUCE:

2 tablespoons olive oil

½ large yellow onion, diced

2 garlic cloves, finely chopped

42 ounces (1.2kg) chopped tomatoes, about 1½ large cans

Flaky sea salt and freshly ground black pepper

1 small bunch of basil, leaves picked off and roughly chopped

TO FRY THE EGGPLANT:

1 cup olive oil

3–4 tablespoons all-purpose flour

1–2 cups bread crumbs

½ teaspoon dried oregano

¾ cup freshly grated Parmesan cheese

3–4 eggs, lightly whisked

TO ASSEMBLE:

7-ounce (200g) fresh mozzarella ball, chopped into small cubes

Flaky sea salt and freshly ground black pepper

2 tablespoons freshly grated Parmesan cheese

1 small bunch of basil, leaves picked off

TO PREPARE THE EGGPLANT:

1 Begin by washing the eggplants and patting them dry with a paper towel or cloth.

2 Cut the eggplant into slices ½ inch (1.25cm) thick.

3 Place the slices in a single layer on a large baking sheet, and sprinkle with a little salt on both sides to reduce the bitterness. Place another baking sheet or cutting board on top of the slices, with something heavy on top to push out more moisture. Cover and set aside for at least 30 minutes.

TO MAKE THE SAUCE:

1 Meanwhile, in a large saucepan set over low heat, warm the olive oil. When the oil is hot, add the yellow onion and garlic, and cook for 4 to 6 minutes or until the vegetables are soft and a little golden.

2 Add the chopped tomatoes, salt, and pepper. Rip 10 small pieces of basil and add to the pot. Simmer for 10 to 15 minutes and then set aside.

TO FRY THE EGGPLANT SLICES:

1 In a large saucepan over medium-low heat, warm 1 cup olive oil.

2 Line a large plate with paper towels.

3 In one shallow bowl, add the all-purpose flour. In a second shallow bowl, combine the bread crumbs, oregano, and Parmesan cheese. In a third shallow bowl, lightly whisk the eggs.

4 Pat the eggplant slices dry. Coat each slice all over in flour, then dip in the egg mixture, and then evenly coat in bread crumbs.

5 Check that the oil is warm enough by dropping in a bread crumb. If it fizzes and bubbles, it's hot.

6 Add the eggplant slices in batches and cook for 2 or 3 minutes per side. Using tongs, transfer the slices to the paper towel–lined plate to drain. Repeat with the remaining slices.

TO ASSEMBLE:

1 Preheat the oven to 350°F (180°C).

2 Spread 1 cup tomato sauce in the bottom of a 9×9-inch (23×23cm) baking dish. Add a layer of eggplant slices, cutting them into the right shape with scissors to ensure the bottom of the dish is fully covered.

3 Scatter a third of the mozzarella on top, and season with salt and pepper. Repeat the layering process until all ingredients are used; there should be about 3 layers of eggplant. Scatter the remaining mozzarella and 2 tablespoons Parmesan cheese over the top, and season with salt and pepper again.

4 Cover with foil and bake for 40 minutes or until the cheese is golden brown and bubbling. Remove the foil for the last 10 minutes or so to add some color to the cheese. Serve hot.

BUON APPETITO, BETCH!

CALAMARI FRITTI

"ka-laa-maa-ree free-tee"

SERVES: 4
PREP: 15 minutes
COOK: 5 minutes

I don't think there's an Italian restaurant that *doesn't* serve calamari. It's a classic appetizer that's served in many non-Italian restaurants as well. Everyone loves it! (Well, okay, not everyone; it can be an acquired taste.) The crispiness and light fish flavor make this one of my favorite dishes. Try it paired with marinara sauce for dipping.

1 pound (450g) whole squid or calamari tubes, cleaned

1 cup cold buttermilk

¾ cup semolina flour

¾ cup all-purpose flour

Flaky sea salt and freshly ground black pepper

1 cup vegetable or sunflower oil

1 handful of finely chopped Italian flat-leaf parsley, for garnish

2 lemons, cut into wedges, for serving

1   Slice the squid or calamari tubes into rings approximately ½ inch (1.25cm) wide.

2   Add the calamari to a medium bowl. Pour in the buttermilk and set aside to soak for 15 to 30 minutes to soften. Remove the calamari from the buttermilk, and pat dry with paper towels.

3   In a separate medium bowl, combine the semolina flour, all-purpose flour, salt, and pepper.

4   Add the calamari to the flour mixture and gently toss until each piece is completely covered.

5   In a medium saucepan over medium-high heat, warm the vegetable oil until very hot. To test to see if it's ready, add a droplet of batter to the pan. If it sizzles, it's ready.

6   Line a large plate with paper towels.

7   Working in batches, fry the calamari rings a few at a time, turning them over with tongs, for about 3 or 4 minutes or until they are a little golden in color. If the oil pops and bubbles too aggressively, turn down the heat a notch or use a splatter screen.

8   Transfer the cooked calamari to the paper towel–lined plate to drain. Repeat with the remaining calamari.

9   When you're finished cooking, transfer the calamari to a serving plate, season with salt and pepper, and garnish with the chopped Italian flat-leaf parsley. Serve immediately with fresh lemon wedges.

TIP *Calamari is usually available in the frozen section at local grocery stores. If you're using frozen, thaw it in the refrigerator overnight before cooking. You also can buy it fresh at the seafood market. Fresh squid should be used within 2 days. To prevent overcooking, work in small batches and take out the calamari when it looks lightly golden.*

BUON APPETITO, BETCH!

IMPEPATA DI COZZE
(PEPPERED STEAMED MUSSELS)

"eem-peh-pah-tah dee coat-zeh"

SERVES: 4
PREP: 15 minutes
COOK: 10 minutes

Can't have mussels without muscles. Just kidding, but this dish is packed with protein and is very easy to make. This is most commonly found in coastal towns of southern Italy and enjoyed with some fresh bread to dip into the sauce. In Italian, we called this *scarpetta*, never letting the sauce go to waste. When it comes to food, Italians are surely resourceful.

4½ pounds (2kg) fresh mussels, purchased cleaned if possible

2 teaspoons freshly ground black pepper

½ cup white wine

Juice of ½ lemon

½ small bunch Italian flat-leaf parsley, leaves picked off and finely chopped

Fresh Italian bread, for serving (optional)

1 Check the mussels, and discard any that are open or cracked. If they need to be cleaned, scrub them with a firm brush to remove any debris. To remove the beard (the hairy-looking string that might be sticking out between the shells), grab it with your fingers and pull firmly until it comes out. Discard the beard.

2 Place the mussels in a colander in the sink, and rinse them thoroughly under cold water.

3 In a large pot with a close-fitting lid over medium-high heat, add the mussels and pepper. Steam the mussels in their own juice for 2 or 3 minutes.

4 Pour in the white wine and cover. Shake the pot to mix the mussels and wine, and cook for 3 or 4 minutes—the mussels should be boiling and steaming inside the pot—until the shells open and everything looks piping hot.

5 Remove the lid, add the lemon juice and Italian flat-leaf parsley, and shake again. Serve hot with pieces of Italian bread (if using).

BUON APPETITO, BETCH!

CLAMS OREGANATA
(BAKED CLAMS)

SERVES: 2–3
PREP: 10 minutes (plus 1 hour to soak)
COOK: 30 minutes

These baked clams are amazing. If you don't like clams, these don't count. *Oreganata* refers to a mixture of bread crumbs, olive oil, garlic, and oregano. This dish is a great party appetizer and is also perfect for the seven fishes on Christmas Eve, which is a tradition in Italy. Get ready to slurp them off the shell.

1½ pounds (680g) fresh shell-on clams, cleaned by your fishmonger

½ glass dry white wine

2 garlic cloves, minced

½ cup freshly grated Parmesan cheese

¼ small bunch of Italian flat-leaf parsley, leaves picked off and finely chopped, plus more for garnish

3 teaspoons chopped fresh oregano

¼ teaspoons chopped peperoncino chili or red chili flakes (optional)

1 pinch of flaky sea salt

Freshly ground black pepper

½ cup panko bread crumbs

1 drizzle of extra virgin olive oil

2–3 lemon wedges, for serving

1 Fill a large bowl with cold water and enough salt so it tastes like the sea. Submerge the clams in the salted water and leave for 1 hour to remove all the sand. It is important to clean the clams really well!

2 Remove the clams from the water and scrub them clean using a firm brush. After scrubbing, rinse the clams under cold water in a colander and leave in the sink to drain.

3 Preheat the oven to 400°F (200°C).

4 Heat a large pan over medium-high heat. Add the clams and the white wine, and allow the wine to evaporate for 1 or 2 minutes.

5 Cover and steam the clams for 5 to 7 minutes or until they are fully opened. Discard any unopened or cracked clams. They will not be safe to eat.

6 Allow the clams to cool for a minute. One at a time, carefully pry open the shells using a fork, remove the cooked clam meat, and transfer it to a cutting board. Dice the clam meat. (Save the shells because they'll be needed later.)

7 In a large bowl, combine the clam meat, ½ of the garlic, ½ of the Parmesan cheese, the parsley, the oregano, the peperoncino/red chili flakes (if using), and the salt and pepper. Add ¼ cup bread crumbs and stir to combine. The mixture should be a little moist and stick together—it shouldn't be too dry or too liquidy.

8 In a small bowl, mix the remaining ¼ cup bread crumbs with the remaining garlic and a generous drizzle of extra virgin olive oil. You will use this mixture later to top the stuffed clams.

9 Separate each joined clam shell into 2 pieces by gently twisting them apart. Place them on a baking sheet, exterior side down, to make little bowls for the filling.

10 Spoon about 1 teaspoon of the clam mixture into each clam shell half, gently pressing it down. Add 1 teaspoon of the bread crumb mixture on top, and a sprinkle with some of the remaining Parmesan. Bake for 15 to 20 minutes or until the breadcrumbs are golden and crispy on top.

11 Remove from the oven and allow the baked clams to cool for a moment before serving. Transfer to a plate with lemon wedges and serve with fresh parsley sprinkled on top.

BUON APPETITO, BETCH!

ROSEMARY FOCACCIA

SERVES: 8
PREP/RISING: 20 minutes (plus 1 hour to rise)
COOK: 25 minutes

My only problem with focaccia is that I legit eat the whole loaf in seconds. Get ready to hit the gym after this one because this is above and beyond your typical bread. I swear there's no secret ingredient making it this addictive. It's just *that good!*

FOR THE DOUGH:

3 cups (340–360g) type 00 or all-purpose flour

1 tablespoon active dry yeast

1 pinch of flaky sea salt, plus more to prepare the baking dish

1¼ cups lukewarm water

3 tablespoons olive oil

FOR THE TOPPING:

8 cherry tomatoes, halved

8 green olives, halved

2 rosemary sprigs, chopped

2 tablespoons olive oil

1 large pinch of flaky sea salt

SPECIAL EQUIPMENT

Stand mixer with bread hook (optional)

1 In a large bowl, whisk together the type 00 flour, yeast, and salt.

2 Slowly add the lukewarm water, a splash at a time, and use your hands or a stand mixer fitted with a bread hook (if using) to knead the dough.

3 Continue to knead until all the water is used and the dough is lightly springy and soft.

4 In another large bowl, drizzle 1 tablespoon of the olive oil. Using your hands, rub the oil around the bottom of the bowl to prevent the dough from sticking. Add the dough to the oiled bowl. Cover the dough with plastic wrap or a clean tea towel and allow to rise at room temperature for 1 hour or until doubled in size.

5 Preheat the oven to 425°F (220°C). Drizzle the remaining 2 tablespoons of the olive oil in the bottom of a 9×13in (23×33cm) baking dish. Sprinkle all over with salt.

6 Transfer the risen dough to the prepared baking dish. Using your fingertips, lightly pull and press the dough toward all four corners so the dough covers the base of the dish.

7 Slowly and lightly press into the dough with your fingers—not all the way to the bottom of the dish but enough to make divots all over the dough.

8 To add the toppings, place the cherry tomato halves and the green olive halves in the divots or anywhere else across the dough. Sprinkle rosemary across the dough and then drizzle the olive oil over the top and finish with the flaky salt.

9 Bake for about 25 minutes or until golden brown.

BUON APPETITO, BETCH!

PRIMI PIATTI

HOMEMADE FRESH PASTA

SERVES: 4
PREP/RESTING: 25 minutes (prep), 30 minutes (resting)
COOK: 3–6 minutes (depending on thickness)

Making homemade pasta used to intimidate me. But once I actually followed my dad's instructions correctly, it was a life-changing experience. Dramatic? Nyah. The first step to tackling any recipe, especially one like this, is not to overthink. The only reason I'm giving such detailed instructions for this process is to be sure you don't miss a thing.

The only ingredients you need to make fresh pasta are type 00 flour (all-purpose flour is okay too), semolina flour (for dusting the pasta after it's cut), eggs, olive oil, and a pinch of salt. The Italian golden ratio of making pasta is $^2/_3$ cup (3.5 ounces/100 grams) of flour to 1 egg.

If you don't have a stand mixer or pasta machine, don't worry. You can make homemade pasta with your hands, a rolling pin, and a knife. (You think we Italians talk with our hands this much and only use machines?) I'll show you how to make and hand-cut tagliatelle, fettuccine, linguine, pappardelle, and lasagna without any special equipment. You can even make ravioli and gnocchi without tools! If you are working with a pasta machine, you can make additional pasta shapes, depending on which attachments you have.

What are we waiting for? Let's make some fresh pasta, betch! You'll never forget taking your first bite of pasta *you* created.

2½ cups type 00 flour or all-purpose flour

4 large eggs

½ teaspoon flaky sea salt

½ tablespoon extra virgin olive oil

½ cup semolina flour, for dusting

HOW TO MAKE PASTA DOUGH BY HAND:

1 On a clean work surface, dump the type 00 flour into a pile. Using your hands or the bottom of a bowl, create a well in the center of the mound large enough to fit all the eggs.

2 Crack the eggs into the well in the flour. Sprinkle the salt and drizzle some extra virgin olive oil on top of the eggs. Puncture the egg yolks with the fork and then carefully whisk the eggs.

3 As you whisk, slowly push in small amounts of the flour with your hands into the egg mixture in the well.

4 Once all of the flour and egg have combined, you can use a bench scraper to continue mixing the flour and eggs together or use your hands to fold the rest of the dough. The dough might seem dry, but trust the process; it'll all combine nicely. It's going to get messy, though. Don't be a betch about it.

5 After the dough has formed, knead it for about 10 minutes. (This step requires lots of strength and patience. *"Patience is a virtue."* —my mother.) To knead, simply press the heel of your hand into the ball of dough, pushing forward and down. You want to really work the dough for a few minutes before adding more flour if you find that the dough is too sticky. Trust the process before you make a sudden change. If needed, you can use a little extra flour on the work surface to prevent sticking.

6 Form the dough into a ball, wrap tightly in plastic wrap, and set aside to rest at room temperature for at least 30 minutes to 1 hour. If you're preparing it ahead, you can place it in the refrigerator for up to 2 days.

KNEADING

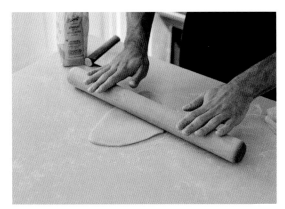

ROLLING BY HAND

Now you're ready to create the pasta. You can make simple and delicious flat pastas like tagliatelle by hand, or if you have a pasta-making machine with attachments, you can make formed shapes like penne.

1 To begin, sprinkle semolina flour all over your work surface. (Semolina will become your best friend in this process.) Cut the dough into 4 pieces and gently knead each into nice, flat rounds.

2 Roll out each piece of dough with a rolling pin until it is thin enough that you can see your fingers through it. (I don't expect you to actually measure it, but seeing your fingers through the dough is a great gauge.)

3 Fold the dough into ribbons, about a fold every 1 inch (2.5cm). Using a sharp knife, slice horizontal strips across the dough according to how wide you want your pasta to be. Unroll the folds, dredge the strips in a little more semolina, and twist them gently into little portion-sized piles until you're ready to cook.

PASTA WIDTHS:

Tagliatelle: 1/4 inch (0.5cm)

Fettuccine: 1/6 inch (4mm)

Linguine: 1/8 inch (3mm)

Pappardelle: 3/4 inch (2cm)

To make lasagna, lay your dough in a baking dish and use a knife to square off the edges so you have a sheet of pasta that fits perfectly.

I haven't included spaghetti because of its round shape. You'll need a machine with the spaghetti attachment to make spaghetti.

CUTTING BY MACHINE

HOW TO MAKE PASTA DOUGH WITH A MIXER:

Kneading the dough with a mixer saves time and effort. I recommend using a stand mixer, if you have one, with a dough hook attachment.

Combine all your ingredients in the mixer bowl, and mix and knead the dough on low for 8 to 10 minutes or until it's smooth and stretchy. If the dough appears dry, add 1 tablespoon of water. If the dough appears wet, add an extra 1 tablespoon of type "00" flour.

Form the dough into a ball with your hands, wrap tightly in plastic wrap, and set aside to rest at room temperature for 30 minutes to 1 hour. Or you can make ahead and refrigerate the dough for up to 2 days.

HOW TO MAKE FRESH PASTA BY MACHINE:

If you want to make pasta with a machine, I recommend the Imperia pasta machine. It's an affordable, easy-to-use starter machine that helps with the rolling process—and it's made in Italy, baby! A pasta maker allows you to choose your preferred thickness and comes with a few attachments for different pasta shapes. You also can use a stand mixer with pasta-making attachments. The process is the same.

To begin, sprinkle semolina flour all over your work surface. Cut the dough into 4 pieces, form each into flat rounds, and roll out thin. Dust with semolina flour prior to rolling and again after it's rolled out.

Pull out and rotate the numbered knob on the side of your pasta rolling machine to adjust the thickness of your dough. Using one rolled out piece of dough at a time, begin with the thickest setting, feed the dough through, and then continue to decrease the size setting down to whichever thickness you desire for your pasta. A perfect finished thickness for most rolled pasta is 1mm.

ROLLING BY MACHINE

DRYING PASTA

HOW TO STORE FRESH PASTA:

If you're not cooking your fresh pasta right away, gently spread it on a baking sheet and allow it to dry slightly for 30 minutes. Then transfer the pasta to an airtight container or zipper-lock plastic bags and squeeze out any excess air. Store in the refrigerator for up to 3 days or in the freezer for up to 2 weeks. To use frozen pasta, thaw it in the refrigerator for 5 hours before cooking as usual.

HOW TO COOK FRESH PASTA:

Before you cook fresh pasta, know that it cooks much faster than dried pasta.

Bring a large pot of generously salted water to a boil over high heat. Add the fresh pasta and immediately stir to prevent the pasta from sticking together. Cook until the pasta is al dente (cooked but still firm to the bite). The cooking time will vary depending on the thickness of the pasta you made. I recommend cooking for 3 or 4 minutes and then taking out a piece to taste-test every 30 seconds to 1 minute until it reaches the perfect consistency.

HOMEMADE GNOCCHI

"no-key"

SERVES: 4
PREP/MARINATE: 40 minutes (prep), 30 minutes (resting)
COOK: 5 minutes

Gnocchi (pronounced *no-key*) are fluffy little Italian dumplings—and one of the greatest comfort foods ever created. Enjoy them with your favorite pasta sauce. As with the homemade pasta recipe, be patient when making gnocchi, and give it as much love as you can while creating it.

1 pound (450g) medium russet or yukon gold potatoes

1½ cups all-purpose flour

1 large egg

1 pinch of flaky sea salt

1 tablespoon potato starch (optional)

SPECIAL EQUIPMENT

Potato ricer or potato masher

1 Clean the potatoes and place them in a large pot of salted water. Bring to a boil over high heat and boil the potatoes for 30 to 45 minutes, depending on the size and number of potatoes, until fork-tender.

2 Drain the potatoes and allow to cool a little until they're easy to handle. Using the tip of a spoon or your fingers, lift and peel away the skin.

3 Dump out the all-purpose flour into a pile on your work surface and make a well in the center. Using a potato ricer, squeeze the potatoes directly into the flour well. If using a potato masher, mash the potatoes directly in the well, being sure to mash them thoroughly. If any chunks remain, they'll cause problems later.

4 Whisk the egg in a small bowl, then and the salt. Pour the egg into the well with the potatoes.

5 Using your hands, bring the mixture together. Knead the dough for about 10 minutes, pressing the heel of your hand into the dough and pushing forward and down. Don't over-knead the dough or it will get sticky. If this happens, add about 1 tablespoon potato starch, not flour, and keep kneading.

6 Cut the dough into 4 pieces. Using your hands, roll each piece into a tube about ½ inch (1.25cm) wide. Be sure to keep your work surface floured while you work.

7 You have a few options for shaping the gnocchi. The first option is to simply cut 1-inch (2.5cm) pillows. You can stop there, or you roll the pillows on a gnocchi board or the back of a fork's tines to create ridges. Either way, let the gnocchi rest for 20 to 30 minutes before cooking.

8 Bring a large pot of salted water to a boil over high heat. Add the gnocchi a few at a time and stir so they don't stick together. When the gnocchi float, they are done. Drain the gnocchi and toss in your choice of sauce. Gnocchi goes great with a sage butter sauce or tomato sauce.

TIP *Potato starch will help bind the gnocchi dough together to form a more firm dough. Potato starch is carried in most popular super markets in the baking section.*

BUON APPETITO, BETCH!

AGLIO OLIO PEPERONCINO
(SPAGHETTI WITH GARLIC AND OLIVE OIL)

"ahg-lee-oh Oh-lee-oh"

SERVES: 4
PREP: 5 minutes
COOK: 15 minutes

This pasta dish is often eaten after a long night of fun or even after a light dinner because it's so easy to make (you may have all the ingredients in your pantry already) yet so flavorful. My twist is adding toasted pine nuts to enhance the rich and buttery taste of the dish. A word of caution: Don't let the garlic burn!

12 ounces (340g) linguine or spaghetti

2–4 garlic cloves, thinly sliced

½ teaspoon chopped peperoncino chili or red pepper flakes

4 tablespoons extra virgin olive oil

½ bunch of Italian flat-leaf parsley, leaves picked off and finely chopped, plus more for garnish

1 tablespoon pine nuts (optional)

1 pinch of flaky sea salt

Freshly ground black pepper

Freshly grated Parmesan cheese, for garnish

1 Bring a large pot of salted water to a boil over high heat. Add the linguine and cook per the package instructions until just al dente (cooked but still firm to the bite). Drain the linguine, reserving 1 cup of the cooking water.

2 In a medium saucepan over medium-low heat, gently sauté the garlic and peperoncino chile in 2 tablespoons extra virgin olive oil for 2 to 3 minutes. Do not allow them to burn.

3 Add most of the Italian flat-leaf parsley to the pan, reserving a pinch for garnishing, and turn off the heat.

4 In a separate medium pan over low heat, toast the pine nuts for 3 to 4 minutes or until lightly browned.

5 Add the toasted pine nuts and linguine to the sauté pan with the sauce, along with the salt and pepper and a splash of pasta water. Using tongs, turn the pasta to coat it in the fragrant oil.

6 Add 1 tablespoon of olive oil and some pasta water, a little at a time, until you have a lovely thick sauce coating the pasta.

7 Garnish with the remaining 1 tablespoon olive oil, a little more parsley, and lots of Parmesan cheese and serve.

BUON APPETITO, BETCH!

PASTA ALLA GENOVESE
(BASIL PESTO PASTA)

"pasta alla jeh-no-veh-seh"

SERVES: 4
PREP: 10 minutes
COOK: 15 minutes

This dish is a vegetarian's dream come true. I can't help but take a deep inhale through my nose to admire the smell of all that basil. I love basil so much, I've considered creating my own basil perfume. A word of caution: Pine nuts burn easily so watch them carefully.

12 ounces (340g) penne

4 tablespoons pine nuts

3 packed cups basil leaves

2 garlic cloves, peeled

1 cup freshly grated Parmesan cheese, plus a little more for serving

1 pinch of flaky sea salt

4 tablespoons extra virgin olive oil

Freshly ground black pepper

1 Bring a large pot of salted water to a boil over high heat. Add the penne and cook per the package instructions until just al dente (cooked but still firm to the bite). Drain the penne, reserving 1 cup of the cooking water, and return the penne to the pot.

2 In a small frying pan over medium heat, toast the pine nuts for 3 to 5 minutes to give them little color (just make sure they don't burn or they'll taste bitter).

3 Wash the basil leaves in cold water and then place them in a bowl with ice for a few minutes.

4 In a food processor, blitz the garlic, pine nuts, most of the Parmesan cheese, and salt at 30-second intervals.

5 Add the extra virgin olive oil and blend for 1 minute or until you get a creamy pesto sauce. Using a spatula, transfer the pesto to the pot with the penne. Add 1 or 2 tablespoons of the pasta cooking water and stir well to make a beautiful sauce.

6 Add the remaining Parmesan on top, season with salt and pepper, and serve.

BUON APPETITO, BETCH!

SPAGHETTI MARINARA

"spa-geh-tee mah-ree-naa-rah"

SERVES: 4
PREP: 5 minutes
COOK: 15 minutes

You won't believe how easy it is to make homemade marinara sauce. Marinara sauce is used in many Italian-American recipes, like Chicken Parmesan (page 183) or Spaghetti and Meatballs (page 143). I have never used jarred marinara sauce and don't plan on it!

12 ounces (340g) spaghetti

3 tablespoons extra virgin olive oil

3 medium garlic cloves, thinly sliced

2 pounds (1kg) cherry tomatoes, halved

3 tablespoons freshly grated Parmesan cheese

1 pinch of flaky sea salt

Freshly ground black pepper

½ bunch of basil, leaves picked off and roughly torn, for garnish

1   Bring a large pot of salted water to a boil over high heat. Add the spaghetti and cook per the package instructions until just al dente (cooked but still firm to the bite). Drain the spaghetti, reserving 1 cup of the cooking water.

2   In a large frying pan over medium heat, warm the extra virgin olive oil. When the oil is hot add the garlic, and cook for 2 to 3 minutes or until slightly golden.

3   Add the cherry tomatoes, reduce the heat to low, and simmer for 10 minutes. For the last 3 to 5 minutes, cover the pan.

4   Add the spaghetti to the tomato mixture and mix to combine. If needed, add a splash of the pasta cooking water to thicken the sauce.

5   Add ½ of the Parmesan cheese, season with salt and pepper, and stir.

6   Garnish with the rest of the Parmesan and basil, and serve.

BUON APPETITO, BETCH!

PENNE ALLA VODKA

SERVES: 4
PREP: 5 minutes
COOK: 23 minutes

Two things I love: pasta and liquor. This dish is loads of fun to make, especially because of the fire from the vodka. But be careful. You might end up with a hangover the next morning if you eat too much.

12 ounces (340g) penne

1 tablespoon extra virgin olive oil

3 ounces (85g) pancetta

½ yellow onion, finely diced

3 cloves garlic, minced

½ teaspoon red pepper flakes

2 cups cherry tomatoes, halved

¼ cup vodka

⅔ cup heavy cream

1 pinch of flaky sea salt

Freshly ground black pepper

½ cup freshly grated Parmesan cheese

½ bunch of basil or Italian flat-leaf parsley, leaves picked off and finely chopped, for garnish

1   Bring a large pot of salted water to a boil over high heat. Add the penne and cook per the package instructions until just al dente (cooked but still firm to the bite). Drain the penne, reserving 1 cup of the cooking water.

2   In a large saucepan over medium heat, warm the extra virgin olive oil. Add the pancetta, yellow onion, garlic, and red pepper flakes, and fry for 3 to 5 minutes or until the pancetta has a little color to its edges.

3   Add the cherry tomatoes and vodka, and cook for 5 minutes on medium heat or until the tomatoes soften and their skins wrinkle.

4   Add the heavy cream, and stir to combine. Reduce the heat to low and simmer, covered for 10 minutes or until the tomatoes are beautifully soft.

5   Add the penne to the saucepan, along with a generous splash of the pasta cooking water, and stir until the water is absorbed and the sauce thickens.

6   Season with salt and pepper, add the Parmesan cheese to the pan, and stir combine.

7   Garnish with basil or Italian flat-leaf parsley and serve.

BUON APPETITO, BETCH!

PENNE CON MELANZANE E RICOTTA
(PENNE WITH EGGPLANT AND RICOTTA)

"pen-eh cone me-lawn-zah-neh eh ree-coat-ah"

SERVES: 4
PREP: 5 minutes
COOK: 30 minutes

The combination of tomatoes, eggplant, and ricotta cheese creates a beautifully creamy, almost pink sauce, in this simple but amazing dish.

1 medium eggplant, skin on

4 tablespoons extra virgin olive oil

1 garlic clove

1 × 28-ounce (800g) can passata, or 1 × 28-ounce (800g) can finely chopped plum tomatoes

Flaky sea salt and freshly ground black pepper

12 ounces (340g) penne

10 ounces (285g) ricotta cheese

½ small bunch of basil leaves, torn, for garnish

1. Rinse the eggplant and pat it dry with paper towels. Cut the eggplant into cubes ½ inch (1.25cm) thick, place in a strainer in the sink, and generously sprinkle with salt. Stir to coat and let sit for 30 minutes to reduce the bitterness. Pat dry before cooking.

2. In a frying pan over medium heat, warm 2 tablespoons extra virgin olive oil. When the oil is hot, add the eggplant and cook for 10 to 12 minutes or until the eggplant is golden brown. Transfer the eggplant to a paper towel–lined plate and set aside.

3. Wipe the pan clean with a paper towel. Set over medium heat and warm the remaining 2 tablespoons olive oil.

4. Crush the garlic with the heel of your hand or the side of a knife. When the oil is hot, add the garlic, and cook for 2 to 3 minutes or until golden. Remove and discard the garlic.

5. Add the passata to the pan, along with a splash of hot water and a generous amount of salt and pepper. Reduce the heat to low and simmer the sauce for 15 minutes to thicken and intensify.

6. Bring a large pot of salted water to a boil over high heat. Add the penne and cook per the package instructions until just al dente (cooked but still firm to the bite). Drain the penne, reserving 1 cup of the cooking water.

7. Add the fried eggplant to the sauce in the pan and cook for 5 minutes.

8. Add the penne and ricotta cheese to the sauce and stir with a wooden spoon just until heated. Do not boil the sauce because it may separate.

9. Garnish with some freshly torn basil leaves and serve.

BUON APPETITO, BETCH!

PASTA E FAGIOLI
(PASTA AND BEANS)

"pasta eh fa-joe-lee"

SERVES: 4
PREP: 5 minutes
COOK: 20 minutes

Pasta and beans might sound weird going together but the combination is perfect and it's the ultimate comfort food. In New York, they call it *pasta fazool.* Don't be a fool and call it fazool... It's pronounced *fa-joe-lee.* Fun fact: The aromatic base of pasta fagioli is minced carrots, celery, and onion sautéed in olive oil is known as "soffritto." Soffritto is known as the holy trinity in Italian cooking.

1 medium yellow onion, diced

1 carrot, diced

1 celery stalk, diced

2 garlic cloves, minced

¼ teaspoon chopped peperoncino chili, or red pepper flakes

4 large canned, peeled Roma tomatoes

6 ounces (170g) cherry tomatoes

2 rosemary sprigs, bundled in cooking twine (optional)

1 teaspoon dried oregano

1 pinch of flaky sea salt

Freshly ground black pepper

1 × 15-ounce (425g) can cannellini beans, with liquid

5–6 cups vegetable or chicken broth or stock

9 ounces (255g) tubetti or mixed pasta

2 tablespoons of extra virgin olive oil

Freshly grated Parmesan cheese, for garnish

1 In a large pot or Dutch oven over medium-low heat, make the soffritto by sautéing the yellow onion, carrot, celery, and garlic together in 2 tablespoons of olive oil for 4 to 6 minutes.

2 Add the peperoncino chili, Roma tomatoes, cherry tomatoes, rosemary, and oregano. Season well with salt and pepper, and simmer for a few minutes until fragrant.

3 In a medium bowl, using a wooden spoon or a potato masher, mash ½ of the cannellini beans with their liquid until the texture is thick and creamy.

4 Add the blended beans to the pot and stir. Add 5 cups vegetable broth, increase the heat to medium-high, and bring to a boil. Add the rest of the cannellini beans and the uncooked tubetti pasta to the pot, and stir. Simmer, stirring regularly and adding another 1 cup of broth if needed, for 12 to 15 minutes or until the tubetti is only just al dente (cooked but still firm to the bite). The pasta will continue to absorb more liquid after the heat is switched off, so don't overcook it.

5 Spoon into bowls, garnish with Parmesan cheese, and serve.

BUON APPETITO, BETCH!

TUBETTI E LENTICCHIE
(PASTA AND LENTILS)

"tu-bet-tee eh len-tee-kyeh"

SERVES: 4 people
PREP: 20 minutes
COOK: 35 minutes

I think I've seen my dad make this dish at least 1,000 times. He's addicted, for a reason. Pasta and lentils are the perfect comfort food and can be enjoyed both on the drier or more soupy side. Healthy, hearty, and full of protein.

1 cup brown lentils

1–2 bouillon cubes

2 tablespoons extra virgin olive oil

1 medium yellow onion, diced

1 medium carrot, diced

1 celery stalk, diced

¼ cup smoked pancetta, diced

1 whole garlic clove, skin on

1 × 15-ounce (425g) can whole tomatoes

2 teaspoons dried oregano

2 cups tubetti

3–4 tablespoons finely chopped Italian flat-leaf parsley (optional)

4 tablespoons freshly grated Parmesan cheese

1 pinch of flaky sea salt

Freshly ground black pepper

1 Place the brown lentils in a fine mesh strainer and rinse under cold running water. Pour them into a medium pot, cover with a good amount of water (or broth if you prefer), and set over high heat. Bring to a boil and cook according to the package directions (usually 18 to 20 minutes) until just al dente (cooked but still firm to the bite). Drain the lentils, reserving the cooking water.

2 In a large saucepan over medium-low heat, warm the extra virgin olive oil. When the oil is hot, add the yellow onion, carrot, celery, and pancetta, and sauté for about 10 minutes or until soft but without too much color.

3 Add the skin-on garlic (in camicia or "with its shirt on" in Italian), tomatoes, and oregano, and stir to combine.

4 Add the tubetti pasta, plus 1 or 2 cups of the reserved lentil cooking water as needed, and cook for 10 minutes. The tubetti will absorb the liquid as it cooks.

5 Squeeze the garlic out of its "shirt," add to the saucepan, and mix well to combine.

6 Add the Italian flat-leaf parsley and Parmesan cheese and mix well. Season with salt and pepper and serve.

BUON APPETITO, BETCH!

SPAGHETTI ALLA NERANO
(SPAGHETTI WITH ZUCHINNI)

"spa-get-ee ah la neh-rah-no"

SERVES: 4
PREP: 15 minutes
COOK: 20 minutes

Originated in the beautiful fishing village of Nerano on the Amalfi coast, Spaghetti alla Nerano is a simple vegetarian pasta that consists of lightly fried zucchini and creamy provolone and Pecorino Romano tossed in spaghetti. It is truly one of my favorite pasta dishes. Garnish with fresh basil or mint!

12 ounces (340g) spaghetti

6 medium zucchini

1 cup olive oil, for shallow frying

1 tablespoon extra virgin olive oil

1 garlic clove

¾ cup freshly grated provolone cheese

1 bunch of basil, leaves finely shredded

1 pinch of flaky sea salt

Freshly ground black pepper

3 tablespoons freshly grated Pecorino Romano cheese

1   Bring a large pot of salted water to a boil over high heat. Add the spaghetti and cook per the package instructions until just al dente (cooked but still firm to the bite). Drain the spaghetti, reserving 1 cup of the cooking water.

2   Cut off both ends of each zucchini and discard. Slice each zucchini into thin, round disks.

3   Fill a large frying pan with olive oil to a depth of about 1 inch (2.5cm), and set over medium heat. To test the oil's temperature, dip the end of a wooden spoon into the oil. If you see bubbles forming around the spoon handle, the oil is ready.

4   Working in batches, fry the zucchini slices until golden brown, turning after 1 or 2 minutes to cook both sides.

5   Line a large plate with paper towels. Using a slotted spoon or tongs, transfer the fried zucchini to the paper towel–lined plate to drain.

6   A few minutes before the spaghetti is ready, set a frying pan over medium heat and add the extra virgin olive oil to warm.

7   Crush the garlic with the heel of your hand or the side of a knife. Add the garlic to the pan and stir. Cook for 1 or 2 minutes to season the oil and then remove and discard the garlic.

8   Add the zucchini to the pan and gently stir to reheat and moisten.

9   Add the spaghetti, provolone cheese, basil, and a splash of the pasta cooking water, and stir to mix.

10 After everything is warmed through, season with salt and pepper, garnish with Pecorino Romano cheese, and serve.

BUON APPETITO, BETCH!

CACIO E PEPE
(CHEESE AND PEPPER PASTA)

"cah-chio eh peh-peh"

SERVES: 4
PREP: 5 minutes
COOK: 10 minutes

Cacio e pepe translates to "cheese and pepper." Fresh black pepper is the kick of the dish, the Pecorino Romano cheese is the salt of the dish, and they combine to make the perfect dish, *betch!*

9 ounces (255g) spaghetti or bucatini

2 tablespoons whole black peppercorns

2 cups freshly grated Pecorino Romano cheese, plus more for garnish

SPECIAL EQUIPMENT
Mortar and pestle

1 Bring a large pot of salted water to a boil over high heat. Add the spaghetti and cook per the package instructions until just al dente (cooked but still firm to the bite). Drain the spaghetti, reserving 1 cup of the cooking water.

2 Using a mortar and pestle, grind the peppercorns roughly. If you don't have a mortar and pestle, place the peppercorns in a zipper-lock plastic bag and pound with a meat pounder or rolling pin until you have a few different-sized pieces of peppercorn with lots of powdered pepper.

3 In a medium bowl, add the Pecorino Romano cheese. Add a generous splash of the pasta cooking water and stir to combine.

4 Return the pasta to the cooking pot (the heat should be off) and gradually add the Pecorino Romano mixture to the spaghetti while stirring. Tongs are useful here.

5 Garnish with a little more Pecorino Romano and another sprinkle of pepper, and serve immediately.

BUON APPETITO, BETCH!

PASTA AL PISTACCHIO

"pee-stack-yo"

SERVES: 4
PREP: 5 minutes
COOK: 10 minutes

Don't be afraid to cook with nuts! Have some nuts! You can buy pre-shelled pistachio kernels in most grocery stores, but if you're using the ones with shells still on, use the unsalted ones, otherwise your pasta will be super salty. Pistachios bring a unique, hardy texture to the dish, and pack on some extra protein! You'll be surprised if you have never tried it, and to those who have, you know the deal ;).

12 ounces (340g) penne

½ cup pistachios

4 ounces (115g) pancetta, cubed

1 small yellow onion, diced

2 cloves garlic, crushed

1½ cups heavy cream

2 tablespoons freshly grated Pecorino Romano cheese, for garnish

Freshly ground black pepper, for garnish

1 Bring a large pot of salted water to a boil over high heat. Add the penne and cook per the package instructions until just al dente (cooked but still firm to the bite). Drain the penne, reserving 1 cup of the cooking water.

2 In a small frying pan over medium heat, toast the pistachios for 1 or 2 minutes or until golden brown. (You should be able to smell them!) Remove from the heat.

3 When the toasted pistachios are cool enough to handle, finely chop them. Set aside ¾ of the nuts in a bowl, and reserve the remaining ¼ for garnish.

4 In a large frying pan over medium heat, cook the pancetta for 4 or 5 minutes or until crispy. (No need for olive oil in the pan; pancetta is a fatty cut of meat.) Transfer the pancetta to a plate and set aside.

5 In the same pan, add the yellow onion and garlic, and cook for a few minutes or until soft.

6 Pour in the heavy cream, stir, and cook for 1 minute.

7 Return the penne to the pan, add the pancetta and ¾ of the toasted pistachios, and toss to coat.

8 Garnish with the remaining ¼ of the toasted pistachios, the Pecorino Romano cheese, and a little pepper, and serve.

BUON APPETITO, BETCH!

TAGLIATELLE AL TARTUFO
(TAGLIATELLE WITH TRUFFLE)

"talia-tell-eh al tar-toof-oh"

SERVES: 4
PREP: 10 minutes
COOK: 35 minutes

I have a deep appreciation for the art of foraging truffles. Truffles are one of the most wonderful culinary luxuries in the world. What comes with this exquisite fungi is the high expense. For reference, one whole black truffle costs a little over $100. So an alternative option is black truffle oil, truffle butter, or even truffle salt! Tagliatelle al tartufo offers a creamy sauce that is similar to alfredo sauce and best when made with fresh tagliatelle (reference to my homemade pasta section).

12 ounces (340g) tagliatelle

1–2 tablespoons extra virgin olive oil

1 medium yellow onion, diced

1 pound (450g) pork sausages, casings removed if necessary

½ cup white wine

1¼ cups heavy cream

1 pinch of flaky sea salt

Freshly ground black pepper

1 whole black truffle, or 2 tablespoons black truffle oil

½ cup freshly grated Parmesan cheese, for garnish

1 Bring a large pot of salted water to a boil over high heat. Add the tagliatelle and cook per the package instructions until just al dente (cooked but still firm to the bite). Drain the tagliatelle, reserving 1 cup of the cooking water.

2 In a large frying pan over medium-high heat, warm the extra virgin olive oil. Add the yellow onion and sauté for 3 minutes. Add the pork sausages and break them into bite-sized pieces using a spatula or wooden spoon. Cook for 8 minutes or until the sausage is browned.

3 Pour the white wine into the pan and allow to reduce for a few minutes. The smell of wine will disappear after it has cooked.

4 Add the heavy cream and season with salt and pepper. Simmer gently for 2 minutes.

5 Add the tagliatelle and use tongs to combine it with the sauce. Add the truffle shavings or truffle oil and a splash of pasta cooking water, and mix for a few minutes more.

6 Garnish with extra pepper and a little Parmesan cheese and serve.

BUON APPETITO, BETCH!

GNOCCHI ALLA SORRENTINA
(SORRENTO-STYLE GNOCCHI)

"no-key ah-la soor-en-teena"

SERVES: 4
PREP: 10 minutes
COOK: 45 minutes

My favorite pizza is the margherita pizza. It's so simple but so perfect! This dish has all of the same ingredients with the addition of gnocchi. This vegetarian dish is baked in delicious tomato sauce with bubbling mozzarella and topped with fresh basil leaves—which create the colors of the Italian flag!

2 tablespoons extra virgin olive oil

2 garlic cloves, minced

2 × 14.5-ounce (410g) cans pomodorini (cherry) tomatoes

1 pinch of flaky sea salt

Freshly ground black pepper

8 ounces (225g) fresh mozzarella ball, roughly chopped or torn

¼ small bunch of basil leaves, roughly torn

1 batch Homemade Gnocchi (page 77) or 1 pound (450g) store-bought gnocchi

⅔ cup freshly grated Parmesan cheese

1 Preheat the oven to 350°F (180°C).

2 In a large skillet over medium-low heat, warm the extra virgin olive oil. Add the garlic and sauté for 1 or 2 minutes or until soft.

3 Add the pomodorini tomatoes, salt, and pepper, and simmer for 10 to 15 minutes, breaking up the tomatoes with a wooden spoon as they cook and soften.

4 Add ½ of the mozzarella and the basil to the tomato sauce and remove from the heat.

5 Bring a large pot of salted water to a boil over high heat. Add the gnocchi and cook for 1 or 2 minutes, if using homemade, or per the package instructions, if using store-bought, until they float.

6 Using a slotted spoon, remove the gnocchi, add to the tomato sauce, and toss to coat.

7 Transfer the gnocchi to an 8x8 inch (20x20 cm) baking dish, top with the rest of the mozzarella and the Parmesan cheese, and bake for 20 minutes or until the mozzarella is bubbling and golden. Serve hot.

BUON APPETITO, BETCH!

MANICOTTI

"mah-knee-cot-tee"

SERVES: 6
PREP: 20 minutes
COOK: 60 minutes

My nonna's nonna (my great-grandmother), who was named Giuseppina, taught her this recipe in the 1970s. Giuseppina grew up in a small town named Avellino in the Campania region of southern Italy. When I was younger, my family and I would gather at my nonna's house on Sundays and indulge in a delicious manicotti followed by struffoli (honey balls) for dessert.

FOR THE MARINARA SAUCE:

3 tablespoons extra virgin olive oil

2 garlic cloves, minced

1 small white onion, finely diced

1 pinch of flaky sea salt

Freshly ground black pepper

1 teaspoon dried oregano

1 × 28-ounce (800g) can whole San Marzano tomatoes

2 tablespoons tomato purée

1 tablespoon finely sliced basil, about 4–5 leaves

FOR THE MANICOTTI CREPES:

1 cup whole milk

4 eggs

1¼ cups all-purpose flour

1–2 tablespoons unsalted butter, for cooking the crepes

1 pinch of flaky sea salt

FOR THE CHEESE FILLING:

16 ounces (450g) whole-milk ricotta cheese

1 cup shredded mozzarella

1 cup freshly grated Parmesan cheese

2 eggs

2 cloves garlic, minced

2 tablespoons chopped Italian flat-leaf parsley

1 pinch of flaky sea salt

SPECIAL EQUIPMENT

Electric hand mixer

FOR THE MARINARA SAUCE:

1   Preheat the oven to 350°F (180°C).

2   In a large saucepan over medium heat, warm the extra virgin olive oil. Add the garlic and white onion, and sauté for 1 to 2 minutes or until soft and translucent.

3   Add the salt, pepper, dried oregano, San Marzano tomatoes, and tomato purée, and bring to a boil. Reduce the heat to low and simmer for 20 minutes.

4   Stir in the basil, remove from the heat, and set the pan aside.

FOR THE CREPES:

5   In a small pan over low heat, warm the milk very gently.

6   Crack the eggs into a medium bowl. Add the warm milk, a little at a time, and use a mixer or whisk to mix until just combined.

7   Gradually add the all-purpose flour 1 tablespoon at a time and mix until all of the flour is incorporated and no lumps remain. You're looking for a consistency that is slightly thicker than heavy cream.

8   In an 8-inch (20cm) non-stick frying pan over medium-high heat, melt the butter, swirling the pan as necessary to coat.

9   Gently fill a ladle ¾ full of batter and pour it into the center of the frying pan, carefully (use oven mitts or a kitchen towel to hold the handle if needed) swirl the mixture to evenly coat the entire bottom of the pan. You may need to adjust the amount of batter you use for the second crepe if it's not quite right.

10 Cook for a couple of minutes until the edges start to shrink away from the edges of the pan a little. Gently lift up the end of the crepe with a spatula to check if it's done. There will be some golden-colored patches on the bottom if it's ready. Flip over the crepe and cook the other side the same way. Transfer the cooked crepe to a plate and repeat with the remaining batter. (You should get about 6 to 8 crepes.)

TO MAKE THE CHEESE FILLING:

11 In a large bowl, and using a wooden spoon, mix the ricotta cheese, ½ of the mozzarella, ½ of the Parmesan cheese, eggs, garlic, Italian flat-leaf parsley, and salt.

TO ASSEMBLE THE DISH:

12 Ladle a little tomato sauce into the bottom of a 9×9-inch (23×23cm) square baking dish to keep the crepes from sticking.

13 Lay 1 cooled crepe completely flat on a cutting board or a large plate, and spoon 1½ to 2 tablespoons of the ricotta mixture onto the top of the crepe. Tuck in the edges and roll the crepe over the filling into a long thin cigar shape. Place the crepe seam-side down in the sauce in the baking dish. Repeat until all the crepes are filled and cover the base of the dish. Check after you make 2 crepes that you won't have too much or too little filling left, and adjust the amount you add as needed.

14 Ladle more tomato sauce to cover the crepes evenly, sprinkle the remaining mozzarella and Parmesan cheese over the top, and season with salt and pepper.

15 Cover the manicotti with foil and bake for 35 to 40 minutes. Serve hot.

BUON APPETITO, BETCH!

PUTTANESCA

"poo-tah-ness-ka"

SERVES: 4
PREP: 5 minutes
COOK: 20 minutes

What do you call an Italian prostitute? A *pastatute*. I am not lying when I tell you that pasta puttanesca roughly translates to "lady of the night pasta." I'll let you do the research on that one. The reason for the name is quite a mystery, but the reason this dish is so popular is well known: It has more flavor than you can imagine.

12 ounces (340g) spaghetti

2 tablespoons capers, drained

4 tablespoons extra virgin olive oil

2 garlic cloves, sliced thinly

5 ounces (140g) Kalamata olives, pitted and roughly chopped

6 preserved anchovies in oil

¼ teaspoon chopped pepperoncino chili, or red chili flakes

1 × 16-ounce (450g) can San Marzano tomatoes, or 2 cups chopped canned tomatoes

1 pinch of flaky sea salt

4 tablespoons freshly grated Parmesan cheese, plus more for garnish

2 tablespoons finely chopped Italian flat-leaf parsley, for garnish

Freshly ground black pepper, for garnish

1   Bring a large pot of salted water to a boil over high heat. Add the spaghetti and cook per the package instructions until just al dente (cooked but still firm to the bite). Drain the spaghetti, reserving 1 cup of the cooking water.

2   Rinse the capers under cold water for 1 minute to remove the excess salt.

3   In a large frying pan over medium heat, warm the extra virgin olive oil. Add the garlic, Kalamata olives, capers, anchovies, and pepperoncino chili, and cook for 3 to 5 minutes or until everything softens and becomes fragrant.

4   Add the San Marzano tomatoes and salt, and simmer for 10 to 15 minutes or until the sauce thickens beautifully.

5   Add the spaghetti and about 2 tablespoons Parmesan cheese to the pan, and toss to combine and coat.

6   Garnish with Italian flat-leaf parsley, pepper, and more Parmesan, and serve.

BUON APPETITO, BETCH!

LINGUINE ALLA VONGOLE
(LINGUINE WITH CLAMS)

"lin-gwee-neh ah-la vone-goh-leh"

SERVES: 4
PREP: 10 minutes
COOK: 20 minutes

This is a classic seafood dish from the Amalfi coast region. Every restaurant serves it, everyone loves it, but not everybody has the confidence to make it. Giving the clams a bath to remove the sand is the most important step. Take your time with this recipe, and be patient for the clams to open and release their delicious juices, giving you a sauce to dip some fresh bread in.

1½–2 pounds (680g–1kg) fresh clams, shell-on (smaller ones are better)

1 pepperoncino chili, or ½ teaspoon red chili flakes

12 ounces (340g) linguine

2 tablespoons extra virgin olive oil

3 large garlic cloves, finely sliced

1 cup dry white wine

1 lemon, cut into wedges

½ a bunch of Italian flat-leaf parsley, leaves picked off and finely chopped

1 Wash the clams thoroughly in a colander under lots of cold running water to remove any sand. Remove and discard any clams with cracked or broken shells.

2 Finely chop the pepperoncino chili, carefully removing the seeds and being sure to wash your hands well after. (The chili is hot!)

3 Bring a large pot of unsalted water to a boil over high heat. (The clams are already pretty salty, so no need to add more.) Add the linguine, and cook per the package instructions until just al dente (cooked but still firm to the bite). Drain the linguine, reserving 1 cup of the cooking water.

4 In a large pan over medium-high heat, add the extra virgin olive oil and let it heat for a couple of minutes. Add the clams, garlic, chili, and white wine. Cover and cook for about 5 to 8 minutes or until all of the clams open. Remove any empty or unopened shells from the pan.

5 Reduce the heat to medium, add the linguine, and cook for 1 to 2 minutes to allow it to soak up any remaining juices. Add a splash of pasta cooking water if needed to create a fragrant sauce.

6 Add a squeeze of lemon juice and a sprinkle of Italian flat-leaf parsley, and serve.

TIP *I recommend using fresh small littleneck clams, but any clams can be substituted. Spaghetti is also commonly used, but linguine is popularly used with seafood. Before serving, try to toss the pasta! Check out one of my pastas videos to see how I toss it.*

BUON APPETITO, BETCH!

PASTA AL TONNO
(TUNA PASTA)

"pasta al toe-no"

SERVES: 4
PREP: 15 minutes
COOK: 15 minutes

Pasta al tonno is a favorite amongst Italians and a staple dish in my childhood. The main ingredient is imported Italian canned tuna packed in olive oil. I promise this is the ONLY time I will use canned fish!

12 ounces (340g) spaghetti or bucatini

2 tablespoons extra virgin olive oil

1 small white onion, finely diced

2 garlic cloves, sliced

½ teaspoon red chili flakes

2 tablespoons capers, drained

2 × 7-ounce (200g) jars Italian tuna in spring water, drained

1 pinch of flaky sea salt

Freshly ground black pepper

Juice of ½ lemon

1 small bunch of Italian flat-leaf parsley, chopped, for garnish

1 Bring a large pot of salted water to a boil over high heat. Add the spaghetti, and cook per the package instructions until just al dente (cooked but still firm to the bite). Drain the spaghetti, reserving 1 cup of the cooking water.

2 In a large pan over medium-high heat, warm the extra virgin olive oil. Add the white onion, garlic, and red pepper flakes, and sauté for 2 minutes or until the onions are translucent with golden edges.

3 Stir in the capers and Italian tuna, and remove from the heat. Gently break up any large tuna pieces with a wooden spoon, but keep them to large, bite-sized pieces if possible. Do not boil or cook the tuna for long; it will be the most tender if it's just warmed through.

4 Add the spaghetti to the pan with the tuna, along with a splash of the pasta cooking water, the salt and pepper, and the lemon juice. Set over medium heat and toss for 2 minutes or until combined. If the pasta looks dry, add a splash of pasta cooking water and mix again.

5 Garnish with Italian flat-leaf parsley and serve.

BUON APPETITO, BETCH!

PENNE CON SALMONE RICOTTA E LIMONE
(PENNE WITH SALMON, RICOTTA, AND LEMON)

"pen-eh cone sal-moan-eh ree-coat-ah eh lee-moan-eh"

SERVES: 4
PREP: 5 minutes
COOK: 15 minutes

Salmon is my favorite fish. It offers so much flavor when it's sourced well, and it only requires salt, pepper, and olive oil to be fantastic. This recipe combines salmon with penne and other complimentary ingredients to produce something wonderful.

12 ounces (340g) penne

1 large garlic clove, peeled

3 tablespoons extra virgin olive oil

1 shallot, minced

3–4 ounces (85–115g) good-quality undyed smoked salmon, broken into pieces

1 cup ricotta cheese

Zest of 1 lemon

Freshly ground black pepper

1 handful of chopped Italian flat-leaf parsley, or to taste, for garnish

1 Bring a large pot of salted water to a boil over high heat. Add the penne, and cook per the package instructions until just al dente (cooked but still firm to the bite). Drain the penne, reserving 1 cup of the cooking water.

2 Crush the garlic with the heel of your hand or the side of a knife. In a large saucepan over medium-low heat, sauté the garlic in the extra virgin olive oil for 30 seconds to fragrance the oil. Remove and discard the garlic.

3 Add the shallot to the pan and cook for 2 or 3 minutes or until it softens.

4 Reduce the heat to low, add the pieces of salmon to the pan, and gently turn to evenly cook all sides, about 2 minutes total. It will become paler in color as it cooks.

5 Add the ricotta cheese, most of the lemon zest, and a generous amount of pepper, and stir gently to combine.

6 Add the penne and toss. Add a splash or two of the pasta cooking water to loosen the sauce and cook for 1 to 2 minutes to just warm it through. Do not boil.

7 Garnish with a generous amount of Italian flat-leaf parsley and the remaining lemon zest, and serve.

BUON APPETITO, BETCH!

SPAGHETTI CON GAMBERONI
(SPAGHETTI WITH PRAWNS)

"spa-get-ee cone gaam-beh-row-knee"

SERVES: 4
PREP: 20 minutes
COOK: 15 minutes

The ingredients in this dish bring the prawn's flavor to life—that's why it's important to use high-quality prawns. Prawns are technically not shrimp, but they are so similar that it's okay to use large shrimp as a substitute if you can't get prawns. Prawns are preferred in this dish because they tend to be sweeter in taste and bigger in size.

28 ounces (800g) shell-on prawns or large shrimp, or 14 ounces (400g) peeled prawns or large shrimp

12 ounces (340g) spaghetti

2 tablespoons extra virgin olive oil

1 shallot, roughly chopped

2 garlic cloves, minced

½ small bunch of Italian flat-leaf parsley, finely chopped

1 cup cherry tomatoes, halved

1 pinch of flaky sea salt

Freshly ground black pepper

½ teaspoon chopped pepperoncino chili, or red chili flakes

1 cup white wine

1 Clean the prawns if needed. Twist to remove the head and then use your fingers to break open the shell at the belly and peel off the whole shell, including the legs. Discard the head and shells. Use a small knife to remove the intestine sac, the black line that runs down the spine; it should come away cleanly. Rinse the prawns in lots of fresh cold water and set aside.

2 Bring a large pot of salted water to a boil over high heat. Add the spaghetti, and cook per the package instructions until just al dente (cooked but still firm to the bite). Drain the spaghetti, reserving 1 cup of the cooking water.

3 In a large frying pan over medium heat, warm the extra virgin olive oil. When the oil is hot, add the shallot, garlic, Italian flat-leaf parsley, and cherry tomatoes, and cook for 5 minutes.

4 Add the prawns and increase the heat to high. Season with salt and pepper, add the peperoncino chile, and cook the prawns for just over 1 minute per side.

5 Add the white wine and allow it to reduce and evaporate for a moment.

6 Add the spaghetti, along with 1 or 2 tablespoons of the pasta cooking water if needed, to make a beautiful sauce.

7 Use tongs to combine all the ingredients and coat the pasta with the light sauce, and serve.

BUON APPETITO, BETCH!

LOBSTER RAVIOLI

SERVES: 4 (32 raviolis)
PREP: 1 hour
COOK: 20 minutes

"Ravioli, ravioli, give me the formuoli." That one's for my *SpongeBob* fans. Lobster ravioli is going to cost you. That's not just what makes it special, though. The flavor will bless your taste buds. Save this dish for a special someone, or splurge and make it with a group.

FOR THE RAVIOLI FILLING:
4 lobster tails, each about 4 ounces (115g), shells on
2 garlic cloves, minced
1 cup full-fat ricotta cheese
Zest of ½ lemon
1 pinch of flaky sea salt
Freshly ground black pepper

FOR THE RAVIOLI DOUGH:
1 batch Homemade Fresh Pasta (page 72)

FOR THE SAUCE:
2 tablespoons unsalted butter
1 shallot, finely diced
½ cup dry white wine
4 tablespoons heavy whipping cream
1 pinch of flaky sea salt
Freshly ground black pepper
4 tablespoons freshly grated Parmesan cheese
¼ bunch Italian flat-leaf parsley, leaves picked off and finely chopped

TO MAKE THE RAVIOLI FILLING:

1   Rinse the lobster tails under cold running water and pat dry with paper towels.

2   Fill the bottom of a medium saucepan with about half an inch of water, set over high heat, and bring to a boil. Add the lobster tails, with the meat facing down in the boiling water. Reduce the heat to low and simmer gently for about 8 minutes or until the lobster turns bright red.

3   Remove the tails from the pan and set aside until they're cool enough to handle. Remove the shell from each tail by gently pulling it apart with the meat facing toward you. Using your fingers, a lobster fork, or the handle end of a teaspoon, remove every little piece of valuable meat. After you've picked out all the tails, finely chop all of the lobster meat.

4   In a large bowl, mix the lobster meat, garlic, ricotta cheese, lemon zest, salt, and pepper. Set aside.

5   On a lightly floured surface using a rolling pin, roll out the Homemade Fresh Pasta dough to 1 mm and divide into 2 sheets. Make sure the bottom sheet of pasta dough can slide across your work surface before continuing. This will prevent the ravioli from sticking to the work surface. Evenly space 1-tablespoon dollops of the lobster mixture across the first sheet, leaving a 1-inch (2.5cm) border all around the outer edges and spacing the lobster mixture about 2 inches (5cm) apart. Be careful not to add too much lobster mixture or the ravioli won't seal properly.

6   Carefully lift the second sheet of pasta and place it over the top of the first. Gently press together along the edges of the dallops of the lobster mixture to release any air bubbles.

7   Shape the raviolis using either a knife, or ravioli stamp, by cutting around each dollop of lobster mix, or pressing the ravioli stamp over top of it, then seal the edges by lightly pressing into the dough, and set aside to dry until it's time to cook.

8   Bring a large pot of salted water on a boil over high heat.

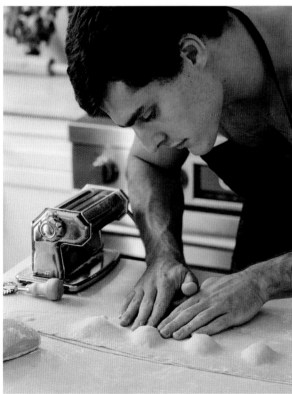

9 Meanwhile, in a large skillet over medium-high heat, melt the butter. Add the shallot and cook for about 2 or 3 minutes or until translucent. Add the white wine and cook for 3 or 4 minutes or until it's reduced by half. Add the heavy cream, reduce the heat to low, season with salt and pepper, and mix gently. Do not boil.

10 Add the ravioli to the boiling water and cook for 2 or 3 minutes or until the ravioli float. Avoid overcooking or the ravioli could start to disintegrate. Drain carefully, reserving some cooking water.

11 Using a slotted spoon, gently transfer the raviolis to the skillet and shake the pan a little to combine them with the cream sauce. Add 1 or 2 tablespoons of the pasta cooking water to create a beautiful, rich sauce.

12 Add some Parmesan cheese and Italian flat-leaf parsley, toss to coat, and serve.

BUON APPETITO, BETCH!

BUCATINI ALLA CARBONARA

"booh-kah-tee-knee ah-la car-bow-nah-rah"

SERVES: 4
PREP: 10 minutes
COOK: 15 minutes

Typically served with spaghetti, carbonara, a classic Roman dish, is one of the most famous Italian dishes there is. This recipe took me at least 10 times to get it right, so follow the recipe to perfection if you want to do it like the pros. Yes, I just called myself a pro. I mean c'mon, making pasta is all I do, people!

12 ounces (340g) bucatini

6 ounces (170g) guanciale

1 large whole egg

4 egg yolks

1 cup finely grated Pecorino Romano cheese

Freshly ground black pepper

2 tablespoons freshly grated Parmesan cheese, for garnish

1   Bring a large pot of salted water to boil over high heat. Add the bucatini pasta and cook per the package instructions until just al dente (cooked but still firm to the bite). Drain the bucatini, reserving 1 cup of the cooking water.

2   In a medium saucepan over low heat, fry the guanciale for about 5 or 6 minutes or until golden and lightly crisped.

3   Remove from the heat. Leaving the fat in the pan, transfer ¾ of the guanciale to a bowl and set aside. Transfer the remaining guanciale to a paper towel–lined plate to drain. This will be used later as a garnish.

4   In a medium bowl, beat the egg and egg yolks. Add the Pecorino Romano cheese and pepper, and whisk well.

5   Add the cooked bucatini to the saucepan in which the guanciale was cooked, set over low heat, and stir to mix it with the guanciale fat. A splash or two of pasta water to create a delicious sauce.

6   Remove from the heat and allow the pan to cool a little. (You're going to add the eggs later, but you don't want them to scramble in the hot pan.) Add the ¾ reserved guanciale and stir in the egg and cheese mixture. Keep stirring, and the sauce will thicken to create the perfect consistency.

7   Garnish with some more pepper, Parmesan cheese, and the remaining ¼ guanciale, and serve.

TIP *Because Pecorino Romano has such a salty flavor, my father taught me to add a few tablespoons of Parmesan cheese to this dish to balance out the tangy taste.*

BUON APPETITO, BETCH!

FETTUCCINE ALFREDO WITH CHICKEN

SERVES: 4
PREP: 25 minutes
COOK: 25 minutes

The authentic Italian *fettuccine Alfredo* is made with only butter and Parmesan cheese. I cooked this dish in the first viral video I created, so this recipe has a place in my heart. Although it is not an authentic Italian dish, it is loved globally for its creamy goodness.

2 large boneless skinless chicken breasts, about 2 pounds (1kg) total

1 pinch of flaky sea salt

Freshly ground black pepper

4 tablespoons unsalted butter

12 ounces (340g) fettuccine

2 cups heavy cream

1 cup freshly grated Parmesan cheese

¼ small bunch of Italian flat-leaf parsley, leaves picked off and finely chopped

1 Season the chicken titties with salt and pepper.

2 In a large saucepan over medium-high heat, warm 2 tablespoons butter. Add the chicken breasts and fry for about 7 to 10 minutes per side or until brown and crispy. Check for doneness by inserting the point of a knife into the thickest part of the chicken. If a little clear juice runs out, it's ready. If there's any pinkness or blood, cook for 5 or so minutes more. Remove from the heat and transfer the chicken to a cutting board to rest.

3 Bring a large pot of salted water to a boil over high heat. Add the fettuccine, and cook per the package instructions until just al dente (cooked but still firm to the bite). Drain the fettuccine, reserving a splash of the cooking water.

4 Using a sharp knife, cut the chicken into slices ½ inch (1.25cm) thick.

5 Wipe out the cooled saucepan with a paper towel and set over medium-low heat. Add the remaining 2 tablespoons butter and allow to melt.

6 Gradually stir in the heavy cream. Increase the heat to medium and bring to a gentle simmer. Add the Parmesan cheese, stir, and cook for 1 minute or until the cheese is melted.

7 Add the fettuccine to the sauce and toss to coat. Reduce the heat to medium-low and gently simmer for 2 minutes while the fettuccine absorbs some of the cream. Add a small splash of the pasta cooking water if needed to loosen the sauce.

8 Divide the fettuccine among 4 plates, garnish with Italian flat-leaf parsley, top with some of the chicken, and serve.

BUON APPETITO, BETCH!

PASTA CON PISELLI E GUANCIALE
(PASTA WITH PEAS AND GUANCIALE)

"pah-stah cone pee-sell-ee e gwan-chah-le"

SERVES: 4
PREP: 10 minutes
COOK: 25 minutes

Thank you, Dad, for introducing me to yet another incredible Italian dish, which I enjoy most as a lunchtime meal. The best part is that you can make this dish in one pot for easy cleanup.

1 pound (450g) tubetti

5 ounces (140g) guanciale

½ medium yellow onion, sliced finely into half moons

6 ounces (170g) frozen green peas

drizzle of extra virgin olive oil

1 pinch of flaky sea salt

Freshly ground black pepper

Freshly shaved Parmesan cheese, for garnish

1 Bring a large pot of salted water to a boil. Add the tubetti pasta and cook per the package instructions until just al dente (cooked but still firm to the bite). Drain the tubetti, reserving 1 cup of the cooking water.

2 Slice the guanciale into long thin strips, about $\frac{3}{8}$ inch (1cm) wide.

3 In a medium frying pan over low heat, cook the guanciale for 5 minutes or until it's crispy at the edges and the fat is released.

4 Transfer the guanciale to a paper towel–plate to drain, leaving the fat in the pan.

5 Add the yellow onion to the pan and cook, stirring occasionally, for 5 minutes or until golden.

6 Add the frozen peas and extra virgin olive oil to the pan and cook for 5 minutes.

7 Add the tubetti to the pan, along with a splash of the pasta cooking water. Increase the heat to medium-high and cook for a few minutes. Season with salt and pepper, garnish with Parmesan cheese, and serve.

TIP *You can find guanciale at your local Italian deli. Call first to ask if it's available; if not, you may have to order it.*

BUON APPETITO, BETCH!

BUCATINI ALL'AMATRICIANA

"boo-kah-tee-knee all amah-tree-chi-ana"

SERVES: 4
PREP: 5 minutes
COOK: 30 minutes

The spice from the peperoncino, the fatty flavor from the guanciale, and the fragrance of the basil create a unique sauce, which is the foundation of one of Italy's greatest pasta dishes. From the city of Amatrice and popularized in Rome, this dish will remain one of my most commonly eaten and loved foods for the rest of time.

12 ounces (340g) bucatini

3.5 ounces (100g) guanciale

1 × 2-ounce (800g) can whole San Marzano tomatoes

1 pinch of flaky sea salt

Freshly ground black pepper

½ teaspoon chopped peperoncino chili or red chili flakes

1 generous splash of dry white wine

1 cup grated Pecorino Romano cheese

1 small bunch of basil, leaves picked off and roughly torn, plus more for garnish

1 Bring a large pot of salted water to a boil over high heat. Add the bucatini pasta, and cook per the package instructions until just al dente (cooked but still firm to the bite). Drain the bucatini, reserving 1 cup of the cooking water.

2 Cut the guanciale into strips and then into cubes.

3 Pour the San Marzano tomatoes into a medium bowl and crush them into small pieces using your hands or a fork.

4 In a large saucepan over medium heat, fry the guanciale dry (without oil), gently moving it around with a wooden spoon to cook evenly, for about 5 minutes or until it starts to crisp.

5 Using a slotted wooden spoon to hold the meat back, remove most of the fat from the pan, reserving enough to coat the pan.

6 Add the tomatoes, salt, pepper, and peperoncino chile into the pan, and stir to combine.

7 Add the white wine, bring the mixture back to a simmer, and cook for 10 to 15 minutes. As the sauce simmers, the wine fragrance will disappear.

8 When the sauce is ready, add ½ cup of pasta cooking water and the Pecorino Romano cheese and stir to incorporate. Just before serving, add the basil.

9 To serve the pasta, use tongs to grab some pasta from the pan and twirl it in the bowl of a ladle or large spoon. Transfer the twirled pasta to the plate and carefully remove the spoon. Garnish with a little more salt, pepper, and basil, and serve.

BUON APPETITO, BETCH!

RIGATONI ALLA BUTTERA

"ree-gah-tony aah la boo-tear-aah"

SERVES: 4
PREP: 5 minutes
COOK: 20 minutes

Believe me when I say that I ordered this dish from my father's restaurants every time for 15 years. The simple combination of the cream sauce, sausage, and peas go together beautifully. Although Italians aren't too fond of using cream, they clearly haven't tried this recipe.

12 ounces (340g) rigatoni

2 tablespoons olive oil

2 garlic cloves, finely chopped

1 pound (450g) Italian pork sausage

1 × 28-ounce (800g) can whole or chopped tomatoes

1 cup heavy cream

1 teaspoon chopped pepperoncino or red chili flakes

1 small bag frozen green peas, about 1 pound (450g)

Flaky sea salt and freshly ground black pepper

3 tablespoons freshly grated Parmesan cheese, for garnish

1 Bring a large pot of salted water to a boil over high heat. Add the rigatoni pasta and cook per the package instructions until just al dente (cooked but still firm to the bite). I always taste the pasta 1 or 2 minutes before it's ready. Drain the rigatoni, reserving 1 cup of the cooking water.

2 In a large frying pan over medium heat, warm the olive oil. When the oil is hot, add the garlic and gently cook for 1 or 2 minutes or until golden.

3 Add the Italian pork sausage to the pan and break it up using a spatula. Increase the heat to medium high and cook the sausage for 10 minutes or until the meat is cooked through and the edges have some color.

4 Add the canned tomatoes, heavy cream, and peperoncino chile, and stir. Reduce the heat to medium-low and cook for a few minutes or until the color turns pink-orange. Allow the sauce to simmer for a few minutes more to reduce and thicken.

5 Add the peas, bring back to a simmer, and pour in the rigatoni, slowly folding it into the sauce. Add a little pasta cooking water as needed to help bind and thicken the sauce.

6 Remove from the heat, season with salt and pepper, and transfer the pasta to serving plates. Garnish with Parmesan cheese and serve.

BUON APPETITO, BETCH!

RIGATONI ALLA RAGÙ NAPOLETANO
(NEAPOLITAN-STYLE ITALIAN MEAT SAUCE)

"ree-gah-tony ah lah rah-goo nah-pough-lee-tah-no"

SERVES: 4–6
PREP: 10 minutes
COOK: 3 hours

The Sunday night classic ragù, or "meat sauce," is done many ways, but the way my father makes it is absolutely the best. No, this is not a biased opinion. I swear. Make it this way, and you'll never need another ragù recipe for the rest of eternity.

3 tablespoons olive oil

1 pound (450g) beef chuck, roughly cut into 2-inch (5cm) square pieces

8 ounces (225g) Italian pork sausage, broken into bite-sized pieces

8 ounces (225g) beef short rib, roughly cut into 2-inch (5cm) square pieces

1 medium yellow onion, diced

2 celery stalks, diced

2 medium carrots, diced

2 garlic cloves, crushed with the back of a large knife

1½–1¾ cups red wine

2 × 56-ounce (1.5kg) cans whole San Marzano tomatoes

Flaky sea salt and freshly cracked black pepper

12 ounces (340g) rigatoni

4 tablespoons freshly grated Parmesan cheese, for garnish

½ small bunch of basil, leaves picked off and roughly torn, for garnish

1   In a large heavy-bottom pan over medium-high heat, warm the olive oil. When the oil is hot, add the beef chuck, Italian pork sausage, and beef short rib, and sear for 6 to 8 minutes or until the meat has color on most surfaces. Transfer to a plate.

2   Add the onion, celery, carrots, and garlic to the pan, and sauté for 2 to 3 minutes or until the vegetables are soft.

3   Return the meat to the pan. Pour in the red wine and cook for 3 to 4 minutes to reduce it a little.

4   Add the Sam Marzano tomatoes, salt, and pepper, and stir to combine. Cover, reduce the heat to medium-low and cook at a consistent simmer for 2 hours, checking and stirring every 30 minutes to ensure it isn't sticking.

5   After 2 hours, check to see if the meat falls apart easily when you pick it up with a fork. If not, continue to cook and check again at regular 20-minute intervals; usually a 3-hour cook time is adequate.

Shortly before the cooking time is up, bring a large pot of salted water to boil over high heat. Add the rigatoni pasta and cook per the package instructions until just al dente (cooked but still firm to the bite). Drain the rigatoni, reserving 1 cup of the cooking water.

6   When the rigatoni is cooked, remove the meat from the sauce and set it aside to rest. Add the pasta to the sauce and stir to combine. Add a small splash of pasta cooking water if needed to loosen the sauce.

7   Plate the rigatoni, adding the meat to the side. Garnish with some Parmesan cheese and basil, and serve.

BUON APPETITO, BETCH!

RAGÙ ALLA GENOVESE
(PASTA WITH STEWED BEEF)

"zee-tee al la jeh-no-vess-eh"

SERVES: 4
PREP: 10 minutes
COOK: 4 hours

This one is worth the wait. The beef will be so tender, it will melt like butter. This Napolitana pasta is truly unlike any other. Yes, I rhymed on purpose.

3–4 tablespoons olive oil

2 pounds (1kg) red or white onions, diced

2 carrots, peeled and diced

2 celery stalks, diced

2 pounds (1kg) beef chuck roast

2 bay leaves

1 pinch of flaky sea salt

Freshly ground black pepper

1–2 cups beef or vegetable broth, as needed

¾ cup white wine

12 ounces (340g) ziti

3–4 tablespoons freshly grated Parmesan cheese, for garnish

1   In a large, heavy-bottomed saucepan or Dutch oven over medium-low heat, warm the olive oil. When the oil is hot, add the red or white onions, carrots, and celery, and fry for 5 to 8 minutes or until soft.

2   Meanwhile, chop the beef chuck roast into medium-sized chunks, about 2 inches (5cm) square.

3   Transfer the onions, carrots, and celery (the soffritto, or Italian holy trinity) to a plate. Add the beef to the pan, increase the heat to medium-high, and sear the beef for 3 to 4 minutes or until it has some good color on most sides.

4   Return the soffritto to the pan with the beef. Add the bay leaves, season with salt and pepper, and reduce the heat to very low. Watch the pan for a few minutes to be sure that the mixture is simmering gently.

5   Cover the pan and cook for about 2½ to 3 hours, checking every 30 minutes to be sure the mixture isn't burning. If needed, add 1 cup of beef broth after 1 hour or so, mix well, and re-cover.

6   When the meat becomes soft and starts to fall apart beautifully (at around 2½ to 3 hours), add the white wine. Increase the heat to medium and cook for 1 or 2 minutes to burn off the alcohol. Reduce the heat to low and simmer for 1 hour. By this stage, the onions should be really soft and melting into a lovely, sticky, fragrant sauce.

7   When the stew (ragù) is almost ready, bring a large pot of salted water to a boil over high heat. Add the ziti and cook per the package instructions until just al dente (cooked but still firm to the bite). Drain the ziti, add to the saucepan, and toss to coat. Remove the bay leaves.

8   Season individual portions, garnish with Parmesan cheese, and serve.

BUON APPETITO, BETCH!

ORECCHIETTE CON SALSICCIA E CIME DI RAPA
(ORECCHIETTE WITH SAUSAGE AND BROCCOLI RABE)

"ore-kyet-eh cone sal-see-cha eh chee-meh dee raa-paa"

SERVES: 4
PREP: 5 minutes
COOK: 25 minutes

The light bitter taste of broccoli rabe and the savory flavors of Italian sausage blended with Pecorino Romano cheese create an explosion for your tastebuds. Orecchiette pasta is one of my favorites because its little pockets capture so much flavor for each bite.

2 small bunches of broccoli rabe, about 14 ounces (400g)

1–2 tablespoons olive oil

9 ounces (255g) sweet Italian sausages, about 3 links

12 ounces (340g) orecchiette

1 clove garlic, minced

½ teaspoon red pepper flakes

½ cup dry white wine

2 tablespoons finely grated Pecorino Romano cheese

Flaky sea salt and freshly ground black pepper

1 Bring a large pot of salted water to a boil over high heat. Trim off the base of the broccoli rabe stems and blanch the broccoli rabe in the boiling water for 1 or 2 minutes. Drain and set aside.

2 In a large frying pan over medium heat, warm the olive oil. If there's a skin on the sweet Italian sausages, remove it before adding the sausage to the pan, breaking it up into small pieces using a wooden spoon. Cook, turning as needed, for 8 to 10 minutes or until the sausage has taken on some color and is cooked through.

3 In the same large pot, bring new salted water to a boil over high heat. Add the orecchiette pasta and stir rapidly for the first 30 seconds to keep it from sticking together. Cook per the package instructions until the orecchiette is just al dente (cooked but still firm to the bite). Drain the orecchiette, reserving 1 cup of the cooking water.

4 Add the garlic and red pepper flakes to the sausage, and cook for 30 seconds.

5 Add the white wine, and simmer for about 3 minutes or until the wine reduces slightly.

6 Using a sharp knife, cut the broccoli rabe stalks and florets into 1½-inch (3.75cm) pieces.

7 Add the drained orecchiette to the sausage, along with a splash of the reserved pasta cooking water, and stir until the pasta absorbs some of the sauce. Taste one of the pieces of pasta to gauge the readiness, and add a little more pasta water as needed. The sauce should be slightly loose; it will continue to come together before it's served.

8 Add the Pecorino Romano cheese, and stir to blend. Season with salt and pepper and serve.

BUON APPETITO, BETCH!

LASAGNA BOLOGNESE

"boh-loh-gnes-eh"

SERVES: 6–8
PREP: 20 minutes
COOK: 3 hours

Tender sheets of pasta, creamy ricotta filling, and a rich tomato and meat sauce? Sounds like heaven to me! Lasagna is the ultimate comfort food that never disappoints. Every Italian family makes it differently, but this recipe will make you fall in love.

FOR THE BOLOGNESE MEAT SAUCE:

4 tablespoons olive oil

1 medium white onion, diced

1 large carrot, diced

3 garlic cloves, finely chopped

1 large or 2 small celery stalks , diced

1¼ pounds (680g) ground beef

½ glass red wine

16 ounces (450g) passata or chopped canned tomatoes

2 tablespoons tomato purée

1 pinch of flaky sea salt

Freshly ground black pepper

FOR THE BÉCHAMEL SAUCE:

4 tablespoons unsalted butter

½ cup all-purpose flour

2½ cups whole milk, plus a splash more as needed

1 pinch of freshly ground black pepper

1 dash of ground nutmeg (optional)

TO ASSEMBLE THE DISH AND SERVE:

1 cup freshly grated Parmesan cheese

12–16 flat lasagna sheets

Flaky sea salt and freshly ground black pepper

A few basil leaves, chopped or torn, for garnish

FOR THE BOLOGNESE MEAT SAUCE:

1 In a large frying pan or Dutch oven over medium-high heat, warm the olive oil. Add the white onion, carrot, garlic, and celery, and stir. Cook for 5 minutes until the vegetables are a little soft.

2 Add the ground beef and season with salt and pepper. Using a wooden spoon, break up any pieces into smaller, consistent-sized pieces, and cook for 5 to 8 minutes or until the meat has a little color to its edges

3 Increase the heat to high, and add the red wine. Stir, and let it cook for 2 minutes or until it evaporates.

4 Add the passata, tomato purée, salt, and pepper, and mix well. Reduce the heat to low, cover, and simmer for up to 2 hours, checking every 30 minutes or so. You may need to add in a little more liquid if it becomes dry.

FOR THE BÉCHAMEL SAUCE:

1 While the Bolognese sauce is simmering, melt the butter in a medium saucepan over low heat. Sift in the all-purpose flour and whisk, making sure no lumps remain.

2 Continue to whisk as you add the milk a splash at a time. Warm gently—do not boil—for about 5 minutes or until the sauce thickens. You're looking for a consistency a little thicker than heavy cream, so add a little more milk if you need to thin it.

3 Add a pinch of pepper and nutmeg and stir. Remove from the heat.

TO ASSEMBLE THE DISH:

1 Preheat the oven to 375°F (190°C).

2 In the bottom of a 9×9-inch (23×23cm) baking dish, spread a thin layer of the Bolognese sauce and then pour a little béchamel sauce on top and spread to make an even layer. Sprinkle some Parmesan cheese over the béchamel and then add a layer of lasagna pasta sheets. Repeat this process for several layers, making sure there's a good amount of béchamel and plenty of Parmesan cheese left for the top.

3 Bake for about 30 to 45 minutes or until the pasta layers are cooked and the cheese on top has some color. Garnish with basil and serve.

TIP *If you want to save some time, you can prepare the Bolognese meat sauce up to 2 days ahead and keep it in an airtight container in the refrigerator until you're ready to assemble the lasagna.*

BUON APPETITO, BETCH!

TAGLIATELLE BOLOGNESE

"talia-tell-eh boh-loh-gnes-eh"

SERVES: 4
PREP: 10 minutes
COOK: 2 hours

Bolognese is simply a "meat sauce." It is my go-to dish when I'm serving large groups of people, or on a date night, with a glass of red wine. The smells will fill the house and even make your neighbors bang on your door for a bite.

4 tablespoons extra virgin olive oil

2 garlic cloves, finely chopped

1 yellow onion, diced

1 celery stalk, diced

1 carrot, diced

14 ounces (400g) ground beef

½ teaspoon ground nutmeg

2 teaspoon dried oregano

1 pinch of flaky sea salt

Freshly ground black pepper

½ cup dry white wine

1 x 28-ounce (800g) can crushed tomatoes

2 tablespoons tomato paste

12 ounces (340g) tagliatelle or pasta of choice

3–4 tablespoons freshly grated Parmesan cheese, for garnish

1 In a Dutch oven or large casserole pan with lid over medium-high heat, warm the extra virgin olive oil. When the oil is hot, add the garlic, onion, celery, and carrot, and cook for 5 minutes or until the vegetables are a little soft.

2 Add the ground beef, nutmeg, and oregano, and season well with salt and pepper. Use a wooden spoon to break up any large pieces of beef and cook 5 minutes more, stirring every minute or so until the meat has a little color to its edges.

3 Increase the heat to high and add the white wine. Stir and let it evaporate for about 2 minutes.

4 Reduce the heat to medium-low. Add the crushed tomatoes and tomato paste and mix well.

5 Reduce the heat to low, cover, and simmer for 1 or 2 hours, checking every 30 minutes or so. You may need to add in a little more liquid if it becomes dry.

6 When the Bolognese is almost cooked, bring a large pot of salted water to a boil over high heat. Add the tagliatelle and cook per the package instructions until just al dente (cooked but still firm to the bite). Drain the tagliatelle, add to the meat sauce, and stir to combine.

7 Garnish with Parmesan cheese and serve.

TIP *Any leftovers can be stored in an airtight container in the refrigerator for up to 1 day. For the best results, add a little olive oil and reheat on the stove over medium heat for 5 minutes.*

BUON APPETITO, BETCH!

SPAGHETTI AND MEATBALLS

SERVES: 4
PREP: 20 minutes
COOK: 30 minutes

Who doesn't love spaghetti and meatballs? It's a classic for a reason. It is our family tradition to use stale bread soaked in milk, which is the secret to making perfect meatballs. To save time on cook day, you can make the meatballs the day before and store them, without the bread crumbs, covered in the refrigerator overnight.

FOR THE MEATBALLS:
3 small slices stale Italian bread, crust cut off
⅓ cup whole milk
8 ounces (225g) 80/20 ground beef
4 ounces (115g) ground pork
2 garlic cloves, minced
¼ small bunch of basil, chopped finely
2 tablespoons grated Parmesan cheese
2 tablespoons Pecorino Romano cheese
2 eggs
1 pinch of flaky sea salt
Freshly ground black pepper
½–1 cup bread crumbs

FOR THE SAUCE:
3 tablespoons olive oil
2 garlic cloves, crushed with the side of a knife
½ medium white onion, diced
36 ounces (1kg) San Marzano tomatoes or chopped tomatoes, about 1¼ cans
1 pinch of flaky sea salt
Freshly ground black pepper
¼ teaspoon chopped peperoncino chile, or red pepper flakes
1 teaspoon dried oregano
¼ small bunch of fresh basil, finely chopped

FOR THE PASTA AND TO ASSEMBLE:
1 cup olive oil
12 ounces (340g) spaghetti
½ cup freshly shaved Parmesan cheese
⅓ cup grated Pecorino Romano cheese, for garnish

FOR THE MEATBALLS:

1 In a small bowl, soak the stale Italian bread in the milk for a few minutes to moisten.

2 In a large bowl, mix together the ground beef, ground pork, garlic, basil, Parmesan cheese, Pecorino Romano cheese, eggs, salt, and black pepper. Massage the mixture with your hands to break down the meat to a smooth consistency.

3 Squeeze the excess milk from the bread and add the bread to the meatball mixture. Discard the milk. Mix the bread into the meat with your hands.

4 Spread the bread crumbs on a plate or tray.

5 Using your hands (wet them first to prevent sticking if you like), roll the meatballs to golf ball size, about 1.5 ounces (43g) each. This will make about 12 meatballs.

6 Roll the meatballs in the bread crumbs until evenly coated and place back on the plate until ready to fry.

FOR THE SAUCE:

1 In a large saucepan over medium heat, warm the olive oil. When the oil is hot, fry the crushed garlic to fragrance the oil, then remove and discard it. Add the onion and fry for 2 to 3 minutes or until soft.

2 In a large bowl, crush the San Marzano tomatoes into small pieces with your hands.

3 Add the tomatoes to the pan and season with salt and pepper. Add the peperoncino chile, oregano, and basil, and stir. Reduce the heat to low, and simmer the sauce for 10 to 15 minutes.

TO ASSEMBLE:

1 In a large saucepan over medium heat, warm the olive oil.

2 Add the bread-crumbed meatballs, and lightly fry on all sides for 5 minutes or until brown. (This is just to sear the outside; they'll cook more in the sauce later.)

3 Add the meatballs to the tomato sauce and simmer for 15 minutes.

4 Gently lift the meatballs out of the sauce and set them on a plate until time to serve.

5 Bring a large pot of salted water to a boil over high heat. Add the spaghetti and cook per the package instructions until just al dente (cooked but still firm to the bite). Drain the spaghetti, reserving 1 cup of the cooking water.

6 Add the spaghetti to the tomato sauce and toss to combine.

7 Serve each plate of spaghetti with $2/3$ of the meatballs and a generous amount of Parmesan cheese.

BUON APPETITO, BETCH!

SECONDI PIATTI

HOMEMADE PASSATA

Nearly every recipe in this book requires some sort of fresh, canned, or jarred tomatoes, tomato sauce, or tomato passata. You might be used to using jarred, store-bought sauce, but try making your own. It's not that hard, and one taste of the tomato sauce you make yourself will convince you.

FRESH VERSUS CANNED TOMATOES

I highly recommend using fresh tomatoes to make tomato sauce and passata, especially when tomatoes are in season. The best fresh tomatoes to use for homemade sauce are Roma plum tomatoes. For a quick, simple, spaghetti pomodoro, I also like to use cherry tomatoes. Fun fact: Cherry tomatoes are easy tomatoes to grow, even for beginners. If you have the space to plant a few, please do it.

You can find fresh tomatoes at your local farmers markets or grocery store. When choosing fresh tomatoes, pick one that has a solid weight for its size, is firm yet soft, and has a nice aroma.

Canned tomatoes have their place, too. You can find canned tomatoes in a few varieties. I highly recommend using San Marzano tomatoes when using canned. Why? Uh, because the Italians say so. San Marzanos typically come whole peeled, crushed, or cubed. When using whole peeled tomatoes, I typically empty the can into a bowl and crush the tomatoes with my hands. A word of caution: They might squirt on you as you work, but that's life. I've never used canned cubed tomatoes; never found a need to.

A common question when making homemade sauce is, "Should I use sugar in my tomato sauce?" A simple answer is no. The sugar will level out the acidity of tomatoes, which vary from tomato to tomato. I have never felt the need to add sugar, nor have many generations of Italians.

WHAT'S THE DIFFERENCE BETWEEN TOMATO PASSATA AND TOMATO SAUCE?

Tomato passata is similar to tomato purée. Passata is made from fresh, ripe tomatoes that have had the seeds and skin removed. It's often used as the base of pasta sauces. Passata typically comes unseasoned, with no salt, pepper, basil, or anything else.

Tomato sauce is made from cooked tomatoes and is pre-seasoned, usually with oregano or basil. This saves you some work but gives you less freshness and flavor in the final sauce.

HOW TO MAKE HOMEMADE TOMATO PASSATA

SPECIAL EQUIPMENT
Food mill

Bring a large pot of salted water to a boil over high heat. Drop in the tomatoes, and boil for about 10 minutes or until the skins begin to loosen. Add the cooked tomatoes to a large bowl of ice water and let it rest for 2 to 3 mins. Remove from the water, peel off the skins, chop off the stems, cut the tomatoes in half, and scoop out the seeds. Add the tomatoes to another large bowl and thoroughly crush them with your hands. Run the crushed tomatoes through a food mill until you're left with a tomato purée. To cook this purée, follow the Homemade Marinara Sauce instructions.

HOMEMADE MARINARA SAUCE

SERVES: 4
PREP/MARINATE: 5 minutes
COOK: 45 minutes

The taste of homemade marinara sauce versus store-bought is mind-blowing. You will never use pre-made sauce again. You won't, right? Right!? You can jar and freeze your sauce and use within six months for the most freshness!

2 pounds (1kg) Roma tomatoes

3 tablespoons extra virgin olive oil

2 large garlic cloves, diced or whole

Flaky sea salt and freshly ground black pepper, to taste

5–10 basil leaves

SPECIAL EQUIPMENT
Food mill

1   Bring a large pot of salted water to a boil over high heat. Drop in the Roma tomatoes, and boil for about 10 minutes or until the skins begin to loosen. Add the cooked tomatoes to a large bowl of ice water for 2 to 3 mins. Remove from the water, peel off the skins, chop off the stems, cut the tomatoes in half, and scoop out the seeds. Add the tomatoes to another large bowl, and thoroughly crush with your hands.

2   In another large pot or a skillet over medium-low heat, warm the extra virgin olive oil. When the oil is hot, add the garlic and cook for 1 to 2 minutes or until golden brown. If you leave the garlic whole, tilt the pan to pool the olive oil at the bottom of the pan and then fry the garlic in the pool of oil. If you dice the garlic, simply sauté it as usual.

3   Add the tomatoes to the pan. Have a lid or splatter screen ready in case the sauce pops. Cook, continuously stirring, for 20 to 30 minutes.

4   Toward the end of the cook time, add the salt, pepper, and basil. Start with a little salt and pepper at a time and add more to your taste. You can't underdo it, but of course you can overdo it; oversalting will ruin any dish.

5   If the sauce gets dry at any point, add some water until you get the consistency you like. If it's too watery, keep cooking because the water will evaporate from the sauce.

BUON APPETITO, BETCH!

GAMBERONI ALLA GRIGLIA
(GRILLED SHRIMP)

"gham-bear-oh-knee ah-la gree-lee-ah"

SERVES: 4
PREP: 30 minutes (plus 30 minutes to marinate)
COOK: 10 minutes

Most Italian grilling is pretty simple and straightforward. In this recipe, the natural flavors of shrimp and the char from the grill pair well together. The classic fresh Italian ingredients of lemon, parsley, olive oil, and garlic complete the dish.

2 pounds (1kg) large shrimp, skin-on and whole

Juice of 2 lemons

¼ bunch of Italian flat-leaf parsley, leaves picked and roughly chopped

2 garlic cloves, minced

2 tablespoons extra virgin olive oil

1 pinch of flaky sea salt

Freshly ground black pepper

1   Place the shrimp in a large colander in the sink. Have ready a cutting board, paper towels, a small paring knife, a pair of scissors, and maybe a cocktail stick or two.

2   Devein the shrimp by looking for the dark vein that runs along the back and gently lifting and removing it using the tip of a knife. Rinse each shrimp clean and pat dry with paper towels.

3   In a medium bowl, mix the lemon juice, Italian flat-leaf parsley, and garlic. Save some marinade as a sauce.

4   Add the shrimp, drizzle with a generous amount of extra virgin olive oil, and season well with salt and pepper. Set aside and allow to marinate for 30 minutes at room temperature.

5   Heat the grill (or a stovetop grill pan or large skillet) to medium-high. Add the shrimp in batches and grill for 3 to 5 minutes per side, brushing on extra marinade as they cook—try to use it all. Watch that you don't overcook the shrimp, though. If the shrimp is curled up tight, it is overcooked. The shrimp should form a C shape when cooked, not an O.

6   Lay the shrimp out on a serving platter and pour extra marinade on top.

TIP *If you don't have an outdoor grill, you can prepare this recipe on a stovetop grill pan. The cooking time will be the same. Just be sure the stove is hot before you start grilling.*

Source your large shrimp from a local fish market or a grocery such as Whole Foods. My preference for this recipe is tiger shrimp.

BUON APPETITO, BETCH!

SHRIMP SCAMPI

"skahm-pee"

SERVES: 4
PREP: 10 minutes (plus 20 minutes to marinate)
COOK: 10 minutes

In little-to-no time, you can blow someone's mind with how easy, fast, and delicious this dish is. With a pretty presentation, this dish can easily mimic a $30 dish at a fancy restaurant. The butter, on top of the other classic Italian ingredients, creates a rich, mouth watering experience.

1 pound (450g) fresh large shrimp, peeled, deveined, tails on

1 pinch of flaky sea salt

Freshly ground black pepper

5 garlic cloves, minced

4 tablespoons extra virgin olive oil

4 tablespoons unsalted butter

1 teaspoon chopped pepperoncino chili, or red chili flakes, plus more for garnish

½ cup dry white wine

3 tablespoons fresh lemon juice

½ cup Italian flat-leaf parsley

1   Add the shrimp to a large bowl, and season generously with salt and pepper. Add ½ of the garlic and 2 tablespoons of olive oil, and toss to combine. Set aside to marinate for at least 15 to 20 minutes, up to 2 hours.

2   In a large skillet over medium heat, warm the remaining 2 tablespoons olive oil and 2 tablespoons butter. When the fats are hot, add the shrimp and sauté for 1 or 2 minutes per side or until the shrimp turn pink. Try not to overcook them. Transfer the shrimp to a plate to rest for a moment.

3   Add the remaining garlic and peperoncino chile to the skillet, and cook for 1 or 2 minutes or until fragrant. Add the white wine and lemon juice, bring to a simmer, and cook for 1 or 2 minutes or until the wine reduces by half.

4   Add the remaining 2 tablespoons butter, return the shrimp to the pan, and cook, tossing the shrimp in the sauce, for 2 minutes.

5   Turn off the heat. Add the Italian flat-leaf parsley and more pepperoncino chili, if you like it spicy, and serve.

TIP *Serve this shrimp scampi with some fresh, crusty bread to soak up all the sauce. Scarpetta is what the Italians call it.*

BUON APPETITO, BETCH!

SHRIMP FRA DIAVOLO

"frah dee-ah-volo"

SERVES: 4
PREP: 15 minutes
COOK: 20 minutes

Diavolo may mean "devil," but you will be an angel if you make this dish for someone. Spicy shrimp is not all that common, which shocks me, because this one is a *banger*, betch!

¾ pound (340g) shrimp, peeled and deveined

Flaky sea salt and freshly ground black pepper

4 tablespoons extra virgin olive oil

2 tablespoons unsalted butter

2 shallots, minced

3 garlic cloves, minced

1 teaspoon finely chopped Calabrian chili, seeds removed

¼ cup Italian flat-leaf parsley, plus more for garnish

1 pound (450g) cherry tomatoes

¼ cup dry white wine

12 ounces (340g) linguine or bucatini

1 teaspoon red chili flakes

Freshly shaved Parmesan cheese, for garnish

1 Season the shrimp with salt and pepper.

2 In a large skillet over medium heat, warm the olive oil and butter. When the fats are hot, add the shrimp and cook for 2 minutes per side or until cooked through. Transfer the shrimp to a plate and set aside.

3 Add the shallots, garlic, Calabrian chile, and Italian flat-leaf parsley to the skillet and cook, stirring, for 2 minutes or until the shallots are translucent.

4 Add the cherry tomatoes and white wine and stir. Reduce the heat to low and cook for 10 minutes or until the wine is reduced and the tomatoes have softened.

5 Bring a large pot of salted water to a boil over high heat. Add the linguine and cook per the package instructions until 3 minutes before it's ready. Drain the linguine, reserving 1 cup of the cooking water.

6 Add the shrimp to the sauce and stir to combine. Add the linguine, the red chili flakes, and two tablespoons of the cooking water and toss well to combine. Increase the heat to medium-low, and cook for 2 minutes.

7 Garnish with more Italian flat-leaf parsley and Parmesan cheese and serve.

TIP *Dry white wine like Sauvignon Blanc or Pinot Grigio are best for this recipe, and be sure to have a glass yourself to enjoy with dinner (only if you're 21 and up)! Canned tomatoes also work well in this recipe.*

BUON APPETITO, BETCH!

ROASTED BRANZINO

"bron-zee-no"

SERVES: 4
PREP: 10 minutes
COOK: 40 minutes

Me and my mother's favorite fish (other than salmon, lol). BRANZINO, BABY! It blows my mind how soft, juicy, and tasty this fish is with the few ingredients it needs. This is the perfect first whole fish if you have never cooked one.

4 tablespoons unsalted butter, at room temperatire

1 tablespoon capers, drained, rinsed, and chopped

Juice of 1½ lemons

2 garlic cloves, minced

1 pinch of flaky sea salt

Freshly ground black pepper

1 small bunch of Italian flat-leaf parsley, leaves picked off and chopped

2 × whole fresh branzinos, each about 1¼ pounds (565g), skin on, but cleaned, descaled, and heads removed (ask your fishmonger)

1 lemon, thinly sliced

1 tablespoon rosemary leaves

2 tablespoons extra virgin olive oil, plus more for garnish

1   Preheat the oven to 400°F (200°C).

2   In a medium bowl, mix together the butter, capers, juice of ½ lemon, garlic, salt, pepper, and most of the Italian flat-leaf parsley to form a smooth, herby paste.

3   Unwrap the branzino and make a cut horizontally into the belly of each fish where the bottom of the fillets meet so the cavity opens a little.

4   Wearing gloves, rub the butter mixture evenly all over the inside and outside of each fish. Open the belly of each fish a little so you can stuff the cavity with most of the lemon slices and rosemary, drizzle in the olive oil, and season with salt and pepper.

5   Transfer to a rimmed baking sheet and place the fish on their sides. Roast for 30 to 40 minutes or until the skin is crispy and the fish are cooked through.

6   Gently flip the cooked fish open. Carefully lift and remove the spine and all of the bones, using a fork and your fingertips to ease them out. Remove the lemon slices and rosemary and transfer the fish to a serving dish.

7   Garnish with a drizzle of olive oil, the remaining lemon juice, and the remainder of the parsley. Serve immediately, using two forks or a fish slice to serve portions of the flaky cooked fish.

BUON APPETITO, BETCH!

SALMONE ALLA SICILIANA
(SICILIAN-STYLE SALMON)

"sal-moan-eh al-la sea-chili-ah-nah"

SERVES: 4
PREP: 5 minutes
COOK: 20 minutes

People tend to comment on the "lack of seasoning" in Italian cuisine, but what they don't understand is that the true seasoning comes from the flavors of the garlic, wine, capers, and anything else that accompanies a dish. This recipe brings a piece of salmon to life with just a few of those simple, flavorful ingredients. That is the magic of Italian cooking. Serve on top of white rice with a side of sautéed spinach (see page 204).

2–3 tablespoons extra virgin olive oil

1 garlic clove, crushed with the back of a knife

½ cup Kalamata olives, pitted and torn into pieces

2 tablespoons capers, drained

1 cup cherry tomatoes, halved

1 teaspoon dried oregano, or to taste

4 salmon fillets, each about 4–4½ ounces (115–125g)

Freshly cracked black pepper

½ glass white wine

¼ small bunch of Italian flat-leaf parsley, leaves picked off and roughly chopped, for garnish

1 To make the Siciliana sauce, warm the olive oil in a large pan over medium heat. When the oil is hot, add the garlic and cook for 1 minute to soften.

2 Add the Kalamata olives, capers, cherry tomatoes, and oregano, and simmer for 5 minutes or until the tomatoes release their juice.

3 Remove the garlic from the sauce and discard.

4 Add the salmon to the pan, and season well with pepper. Pour the white wine over the top, and simmer gently, covered, for 10 to 12 minutes or until the salmon begins to break apart into several pieces and it's cooked through in the middle.

5 Garnish with Italian flat-leaf parsley and more pepper and serve.

TIP *Spending a few extra dollars for better-quality salmon is worth far more than its price. Good-quality salmon will be juicer and easier to cook and has an overall better taste.*

BUON APPETITO, BETCH!

BACCALÀ ALLA LIVORNESE
(SALTED COD)

"bah-cah-lah al-la leave-or-neh-seh"

SERVES: 4
PREP: 20 minutes (plus 2 days minimum to desalt)
ACTIVE: 1 hour

Baccalà alla Livornese is salted cod braised with potatoes and tomato sauce from the city of Livorno. The cod used in this recipe is heavily salted for preservation, so it needs to be soaked before it's cooked to remove some of the salt. The tomato sauce and cod create a balanced dish you can easily prepare at home.

10 ounces (285g) salted cod, either 1 single piece or fillets

6–8 tablespoons extra virgin olive oil

2 garlic cloves, half crushed with the side of a knife

1 medium yellow onion, finely sliced

14 ounces (400g) tomato passata, or Homemade Passata (page 150)

1 pinch of flaky sea salt

¾ cup all-purpose flour, for dusting cod

Freshly ground black pepper

½ cup dry white wine

2 large yellow potatoes, peeled and cubed

¼ bunch of Italian flat-leaf parsley, leaves picked off and finely chopped, for garnish

1   Salted cod absolutely must be desalted before cooking. The process takes a couple of days, but it's quite simple. If you have one large piece of cod, cut it into several smaller pieces using kitchen scissors. Rinse the fish in plenty of fresh cold running water, and place it in a large bowl or glass dish with a lid. Cover the fish with a generous amount of water, and soak it for at least 2 days in the fridge before using. Every 8 to 12 hours or so, discard the water, rinse the fish, and repeat the soak. After 2 days, rinse the cod a final time and pat dry with a kitchen towel.

2   In a medium saucepan with a lid over medium heat, warm 3 or 4 tablespoons extra virgin olive oil. Add the garlic and the yellow onion and fry for 1 or 2 minutes.

3   Add 2 tablespoons of water to the pan and cover. Reduce the heat to low and cook for about 5 minutes or until the onion has softened.

4   Add the tomato passata and a solid pinch of salt. Stir, cover, and cook for 15 minutes.

5   Place the flour in a shallow bowl.

6   Cut the desalted cod into 2-inch (5cm) pieces. (No need to remove the skin.) Gently dip each piece in the flour to coat and then set aside on a plate.

7   In a large Dutch oven or deep saucepan with a lid over medium-low heat, warm the remaining 3 or 4 tablespoons of oil. Add the floured fish and fry for 5 to 8 minutes, gently turning with tongs to evenly brown on all sides.

8   Season well with pepper and add the white wine. Increase the heat to medium-high and cook for 1 minute to allow the wine to evaporate.

9   Remove the garlic from the tomato sauce and add the sauce to the pan of cod. Cover, reduce the heat to medium-low, and simmer for about 15 minutes.

10 Add the yellow potatoes to the pan. Cover, reduce the heat to low, and cook for about 25 minutes or until the sauce has reduced and the potatoes are soft. Stir the fish gently to avoid breaking up the pieces.

11 Remove from the heat, garnish with 2 tablespoons Italian flat-leaf parsley, and serve hot.

TIP *Store any leftovers in an airtight container in the refrigerator for up to 2 days.*

BUON APPETITO, BETCH!

PESCE ALL'ACQUA PAZZA
(FISH IN CRAZY WATER)

"peh-shheh al-ah-cuah paat-zah"

SERVES: 4–6
PREP: 5 minutes
COOK: 25 minutes

The spirit of Italian cooking is taking a few simple ingredients and turning them into something special. *Pesce all'acqua pazza* translates to "fish in crazy water" because fishermen originally cooked the fish in seawater and wine.

2 tablespoons extra virgin olive oil

3 garlic cloves, roughly sliced

1 teaspoon red pepper flakes (optional)

2 cups cherry tomatoes, halved

1 cup Kalamata olives, pitted and roughly chopped

½ cup white wine

6 small or medium sea bream fillets, or firm whitefish of choice

1 pinch of flaky sea salt

Freshly ground black pepper

1 small bunch of Italian flat-leaf parsley, leaves picked off and roughly chopped

1–2 knobs of unsalted butter

1   In a large, deep skillet (choose one that can snugly fit all of the fillets lying flat) over medium heat, warm the olive oil. When the oil is hot, add the garlic and red pepper flakes (if using) and sauté for 1 or 2 minutes.

2   Add the cherry tomatoes and Kalamata olives and cook for a few minutes or until softened.

3   Add the white wine and allow it to reduce for 1 or 2 minutes.

4   Arrange the sea bream fillets flat in the pan and add just enough water to come about ⅓ of the way up the fish; this will poach it beautifully.

5   Season with a little salt and a lot of pepper and sprinkle ½ of the Italian flat-leaf parsley over the top.

6   Partially cover, reduce the heat to medium-low, and simmer for between 10 and 20 minutes or until the fish is cooked through. The exact time depends on the size and thickness of the fillets. Test for doneness by gently teasing apart a flake or two of the fish in the thickest part of the fillet and checking the color. It should be a solid white color, not at all translucent.

7   The liquid will reduce as the fish cooks to create a delicious, pale-orange sauce. Just before serving, add the butter and allow it to melt into the sauce.

8   Garnish with some of the remaining parsley for a touch of color and serve.

BUON APPETITO, BETCH!

CIOPPINO

"chee-oh-pee-no"

SERVES: 6–8
PREP: 10 minutes
COOK: 55 minutes

TOO MUCH PROTEIN? NEVER! Cioppino is known as THE "fisherman's stew" because it's a crazy combo of a bunch of different fish. Use whatever seafood you want, but this is my way! The only thing I ask of you is to get the fish fresh... It will make or break this dish.

3-4 tablespoons extra virgin olive oil

1 medium fennel bulb, chopped into ½ inch pieces

2 shallots, finely diced

1 pinch of flaky sea salt

Freshly ground black pepper

4 garlic cloves, finely chopped

½ teaspoon chopped peperoncino chili, or red chili flakes, plus more for garnish

3 tablespoons tomato paste

1 cup dry white wine

4 cups fish or chicken broth

1 × 28-ounce (800g) can crushed San Marzano tomatoes

2 bay leaves

1 dozen mussels, scrubbed and debearded

1 dozen clams, scrubbed

1 pound (450g) uncooked peeled shrimp

1½ pounds (680g) fresh halibut or other whitefish, skin removed and cut into 1-inch (2.5cm) pieces

¾ pound (340g) scallops

½ cup chopped Italian flat-leaf parsley, for garnish

Juice of ½ lemon, for garnish

1   In a large Dutch oven or deep-sided saucepan over medium heat, warm the olive oil. When the oil is hot, add the fennel, shallots, salt, and pepper, and fry for 5 to 7 minutes or until the vegetables soften a little. Add the garlic and peperoncino chile and fry for 1 minute.

2   Add the tomato paste and stir to combine. Add the white wine and fish broth and simmer for 2 minutes.

3   Add the San Marzano tomatoes and bay leaves and stir well to combine. Reduce the heat to medium-low, cover, and cook for about 30 minutes.

4   Just before the sauce is done, rinse the mussels and clams in lots of cold water. Discard any that are open or cracked; they will not be safe to eat.

5   Add the mussels and clams to the pan, increase the heat to medium-high, and bring to a vigorous simmer. Cover and cook for about 5 minutes or until the clams and mussels open. Discard any clams or mussels that do not open; they also will not be safe to eat.

6   Add the shrimp, halibut, and scallops. Reduce the heat to medium-low and simmer for 10 to 12 minutes or until cooked through and the clams are wide open. Avoid stirring the stew too much because this will break up the pieces of fish.

7   Remove the bay leaves. Taste the stew and add a little more seasoning if necessary. Garnish with Italian flat-leaf parsley, a squeeze of fresh lemon juice, and some red pepper flakes if you like, and serve.

BUON APPETITO, BETCH!

RISOTTO ALLA MARE E MONTI
(MOUNTAINS AND SEA RISOTTO)

"ree-sow-toe ah la mah-reh eh moan-tee"

SERVES: 4
PREP: 5 minutes
COOK: 40 minutes

Making risotto is a labor of love and patience, but with this creamy combo of flavors from the mountains and the sea (*mare e monti*), it will be worth your while. Risotto is traditionally topped with fresh Parmesan cheese but *definitely not* when it includes seafood. That's a no-no for Italians.

6–8 cups vegetable or fish broth or stock

2 tablespoons extra virgin olive oil

2 tablespoons unsalted butter

1 yellow onion, diced

½ small bunch of Italian flat-leaf parsley, leaves picked off and stalks finely chopped

8 ounces (225g) fresh porcini mushrooms, sliced

1½ cups Arborio rice

1 cup dry white wine

12 ounces (340g) fresh or frozen medium shrimp, peeled and deveined

Sea salt and freshly ground black pepper

2 handfuls of arugula

1   In a large saucepan over high heat, bring the vegetable broth to a boil. Reduce heat to low and gently simmer.

2   In a separate large saucepan over medium-low heat, warm the olive oil and 1 tablespoon butter. Add the yellow onion and Italian flat-leaf parsley stalks and gently fry for about 5 minutes or until soft.

3   Add the porcini mushrooms and gently stir with a wooden spoon.

4   Add the Arborio rice, lightly stir, and cook for 1 minute to coat it in the fragrant oil.

5   Add the white wine, stir, and allow it to soak into the mushrooms and rice for 2 or 3 minutes.

6   Add a ladleful of hot broth from the pot and stir. After the rice has absorbed the broth, repeat this step until most of the stock has been incorporated and the rice is just becoming al dente (cooked but still firm to the bite), about 20 to 25 minutes. This step is a key component in making risotto; you must wait until the stock has been completely absorbed by the rice before adding more.

7   Add the shrimp and the remaining 1 tablespoon butter and cook for 3 to 5 minutes or until the butter is melted and the shrimp is opaque.

8   Serve with cracked black pepper, a small handful of arugula, and a sprinkle of parsley leaves.

BUON APPETITO, BETCH!

CHICKEN PICCATA

"pee-kah-tah"

SERVES: 4
PREP: 10 minutes
COOK: 10 minutes

Go grab some chicken titties from the market and let's make some chicken piccata! *Questa ricetta è la migliore.* Little Italian lesson for you. That means this recipe is the best for piccata. Buttery, lemony chicken and topped with capers, I guarantee you won't be disappointed.

2 large boneless skinless chicken breasts, about 2 pounds (1kg) total

Flaky sea salt and freshly ground black pepper

¾ cup all-purpose flour, for coating the chicken

4 tablespoons unsalted butter

2 tablespoons extra virgin olive oil

½ cup dry white wine

2 tablespoons capers, drained and rinsed

2 tablespoons lemon juice

1 handful of finely chopped Italian flat-leaf parsley, for garnish

SPECIAL EQUIPMENT
Meat pounder

1 Slice each chicken breast in half horizontally, as if you were butterflying it, and then separate it into 2 pieces (4 total). Cover with parchment paper and gently pound each piece with a meat pounder or a rolling pin until it's an even ¼ inch (0.5cm) thick.

2 Season the breasts with salt and pepper and set aside.

3 In a large shallow bowl, pour the flour.

4 Lightly dip and dredge each chicken breast in the flour, shaking off any excess.

5 In a large skillet over medium-high heat, melt 2 tablespoons butter with the olive oil. Add the floured chicken pieces and cook for 3 minutes per side or until browned. (The trick here is to cook the chicken quickly over a high heat to ensure it's well browned before making the sauce.)

6 Reduce the heat to medium and add the remaining 2 tablespoons butter. Add the white wine, capers, and lemon juice, and simmer for 2 or 3 minutes to create a lovely, rich sauce.

7 Using tongs, transfer the chicken to serving plates. Spoon the sauce over the top, garnish with Italian flat-leaf parsley, and serve.

BUON APPETITO, BETCH!

CHICKEN MARSALA

"mar-saa-laa"

SERVES: 4
PREP: 15 minutes
COOK: 15 minutes

I fucking love wine. Am I too young to be saying this? But marsala wine is not your average wine. Let's just say it's way better to cook than drink, but to each their own. The wine reduces to make this thick, savory sauce, that goes so well with the mushrooms.

2 large boneless skinless chicken breasts, about 2 pounds (1kg) total

1 pinch of flaky sea salt

Freshly ground black pepper

½ cup all-purpose flour, plus more to thicken sauce

4 tablespoons extra virgin olive oil

2 garlic cloves, minced

2 cups sliced baby bella or cremini mushrooms

½ cup dry white marsala wine

2 tablespoons unsalted butter

¼ bunch of Italian flat-leaf parsley, leaves picked off and finely chopped, for garnish

SPECIAL EQUIPMENT

Meat pounder

1   Slice each chicken breast in half horizontally, as if you were butterflying it, and then separate it into 2 pieces (4 total). Cover with parchment paper and gently pound each piece with a meat pounder or a rolling pin until it's an even ¼ inch (0.5cm) thick.

2   Season each piece well with salt and pepper and set aside.

3   Add the all-purpose flour to a large shallow bowl. Dredge each chicken breast in the flour, shaking off the excess, and set aside.

4   In a large skillet over medium-high heat, warm 2 tablespoons extra virgin olive oil. When the oil is hot, add the chicken, and cook for just 3 minutes per side or until browned. Transfer the chicken to a plate to rest.

5   Add the remaining 2 tablespoons of olive oil to the skillet. Add the garlic, and cook for 30 seconds. Add the baby bella mushrooms and sauté for a few minutes. Add the white marsala wine, and let it reduce for 1 or 2 minutes.

6   Add the butter and swirl the pan to melt. This will create a tasty sauce with the mushrooms. If necessary, add 1 tablespoon of flour or a splash of water to thicken or thin the sauce as needed.

7   Return the chicken to the pan and simmer gently, using a spoon to coat the chicken with the sauce. Cover and cook for just 2 minutes more. Do not overcook.

8   Garnish with Italian flat-leaf parsley and serve warm.

BUON APPETITO, BETCH!

CHICKEN SCARPARIELLO

"sca-pahr-iello"

SERVES: 4
PREP: 20 minutes
COOK: 40 minutes

This dish is the juiciest, most vibrant, most mouthwatering dish in all of existence. The red bell peppers, the herbs, the chicken, the sausage—oh, *c'mon!* It's the perfect family meal. No kids? Call your friends. No friends? Go on craigslist. (Please don't do that.)

4 boneless, skin-on chicken thighs, about 2 pounds (1kg) total

1 pinch of flaky sea salt

Freshly ground black pepper

4 tablespoons extra virgin olive oil

1 medium yellow onion, sliced lengthwise

4 garlic cloves, sliced finely

4 small pimientos, hot cherry, or peppadew peppers, halved

1 medium red bell pepper, de-stemmed, de-seeded, and sliced lengthwise

½ cup dry white wine

2 × 7-ounce (200g) links sweet Italian sausage

2 × 7-ounce (200g) links spicy Italian sausage

½ small bunch of Italian flat-leaf parsley, leaves picked off and chopped, for garnish

1 Preheat the oven to 400°F (200°C).

2 Pat the chicken thighs dry with a paper towel and season well with salt and pepper.

3 In a large frying pan over medium-high heat, warm 2 tablespoons extra virgin olive oil. When the oil is hot, add the chicken, skin side down, and sear for 3 to 5 minutes per side or until browned. Transfer the chicken to a plate and set aside.

4 Add the onion and garlic to the pan and sauté until golden. Add the pimientos and bell pepper and cook for a few minutes or until golden. Add a pinch of salt.

5 Add the white wine and cook for about 3 minutes or until reduced.

6 In a separate medium pan, warm the remaining 2 tablespoons of olive oil. When the oil is hot, add the sweet Italian sausage and spicy Italian sausage, and cook, turning regularly with tongs, for 4 minutes per side or until lightly browned all over. Transfer the sausages to a paper towel–lined plate and allow to cool. Cut the sausage diagonally into thirds.

7 In a deep, oven-safe baking dish, mix the chicken thighs, sausages, and sautéed vegetables, and spread into an even layer.

8 Cook uncovered for 30 to 40 minutes, stirring after about 20 minutes to ensure nothing sticks.

9 Remove from the oven, garnish with Italian flat-leaf parsley, and serve with a side of patate al forno (see page 209).

BUON APPETITO, BETCH!

POLLO ALLA CACCIATORA
(HUNTER-STYLE CHICKEN)

"pough-low al-la catch-ya-tour-ah"

SERVES: 4
PREP: 10 minutes
COOK: 45 minutes

This version of pollo alla cacciatora is my nonna Italia's recipe. Alla cacciatore in Italian is known as "hunters' style." Although this is a classic dish, everyone has their own twist, but nothing beats the special touch of a grandmother's cooking. This is the perfect comfort food and can be made in one pot.

1 cup cherry tomatoes, halved

3 garlic cloves, finely chopped

1 white onion, roughly sliced into small wedges

½ cup white wine

1–2 fresh rosemary sprigs

2 teaspoons dried oregano

1 pound (450g) baby yellow potatoes, halved

1 pinch of flaky sea salt

Freshly ground black pepper

8 chicken drumsticks, skin on

1   Preheat the oven to 375°F (190°C).

2   In a large, deep, glass baking dish or a Dutch oven, combine the cherry tomatoes, garlic, white onion, white wine, rosemary, oregano, baby yellow potatoes, salt, and pepper. Add the chicken legs on top so the skin is exposed to the heat.

3   Roast, uncovered, for 30 minutes. Remove from the oven and mix well, adding a little splash of water if necessary to prevent sticking.

4   Roast for 15 minutes more, covered if needed to retain the moisture, until the chicken and potatoes are nice and golden brown.

5   Salt to taste and serve warm.

BUON APPETITO, BETCH!

CONIGLIO ALL'ISCHITANA
(ISCHIAN RABBIT STEW)

"co-knee-leo al eesh-kia-tah-nah"

SERVES: 4
PREP: 10 minutes
COOK: 50 minutes

Rabbit? Yes it's true. The island of Ischia, where my dad is from, is home to wild rabbits that have been hunted for centuries by the locals and have become a true culinary tradition for the island. Coniglio all'ischitana is a well-known rabbit stew that I like to say "tastes like chicken," but it truly has its own unique taste and is popularly served around Easter on the island. Patience is a key ingredient to this recipe and the quality of the rabbit.

1 skinned rabbit, cut into pieces by the butcher, about 1½–2 pounds (680g–1kg)

1 cup white wine, plus more for rinsing

4 tablespoons extra virgin olive oil

2 whole garlic cloves

1 teaspoon chopped peperoncino chili, or red chili flakes

½ cup cherry tomatoes, halved

1 pinch of flaky sea salt

Freshly ground black pepper

1 Rinse the rabbit pieces with a little white wine.

2 In a Dutch oven or large, deep saucepan over medium heat, warm the extra virgin olive oil. When the oil is hot, add the garlic and pepperoncino chili and fry for 1 or 2 minutes or until golden.

3 Add the rabbit pieces and sear for 10 minutes or until there is some good color on all sides. Add the remaining 1 cup white wine, stir to combine, and allow the wine to evaporate for about 2 minutes.

4 Add the cherry tomatoes and season well with salt and pepper. Reduce the heat to low, cover, and simmer for 40 minutes, turning the pieces occasionally to avoid sticking. As it cooks, the rabbit will take on a lovely, thick, golden brown–colored sauce.

5 Remove from heat, salt to taste, and serve.

TIP *Finding rabbit in a grocery store can be difficult. If you have trouble sourcing one, try ordering it online from a specialized distributor. (Please don't take your neighbor's bunny.)*

BUON APPETITO, BETCH!

CHICKEN PARMESAN

SERVES: 4
PREP: 10 minutes
COOK: 40 minutes

Why did the spaghetti miss his field trip? He lost his Parmesan slip! I can cook chicken parm with my eyes closed. It never fails to delight me when I take it out of the oven, cut right through the chicken with just a fork, and everything melts in my mouth. Is it possibly America's favorite Italian-American dish? I know there are families in Italy who secretly eat this.

FOR THE SAUCE:

2 tablespoons extra virgin olive oil

3 garlic cloves, finely chopped

1 × 24-ounce (680g) can crushed San Marzano tomatoes

1 pinch of flaky sea salt

Freshly ground black pepper

1 tablespoon chopped basil

FOR THE BREAD-CRUMBED CHICKEN:

½ cup all-purpose flour

2 egg yolks

1½ cups Italian bread crumbs

2 large chicken breasts about 2 pounds (1kg) total, each cut in half lengthwise down the middle to create 2 thin, flat fillets

1 pinch of flaky sea salt

Freshly ground black pepper

4 tablespoons olive oil

TO ASSEMBLE AND BAKE:

8 ounces (225g) fresh mozzarella ball, torn into pieces

½ cup freshly grated Parmesan cheese

FOR THE SAUCE:

1 In a large pan over medium-low heat, warm the olive oil. When the oil is hot, add the garlic and sauté until slightly golden.

2 Add the San Marzano tomatoes, season well with salt and pepper, and add the basil. Cover and cook, stirring occasionally, for 15 to 20 minutes.

FOR THE BREAD-CRUMBED CHICKEN:

1 Preheat the oven to 375°F (190°C).

2 In one shallow bowl, add the all-purpose flour. In a second shallow bowl, lightly whisk the egg yolks. In a third shallow bowl, add the Italian bread crumbs.

3 Season the chicken breasts with salt and pepper. Dredge the chicken breasts first in the flour, then into the egg mixture, and then into the bread crumbs, ensuring all surfaces are evenly coated.

4 In a large shallow frying pan over medium-high heat, warm the olive oil. Add the chicken and fry for 4 to 6 minutes or until golden brown on both sides. Transfer to a paper towel–lined plate.

TO ASSEMBLE AND BAKE:

1 Spread ½ of the tomato sauce into the bottom of a 9x9 inch (23x23cm) baking dish. Layer the chicken breasts on top. Pour the rest of the sauce over the chicken and top with the mozzarella and Parmesan cheese.

2 Bake for 20 to 25 minutes or until the cheeses are lightly bubbling and brown. Serve warm.

TIP *Chicken parm is delicious served on top of pasta, or you can make it into a sandwich. For the best flavor and meltability, use fresh mozzarella and Parmesan cheese instead of the pre-shredded packaged versions if you can.*

BUON APPETITO, BETCH!

VEAL SCALLOPINI

SERVES: 4
PREP: 20 minutes
COOK: 15 minutes

Simple enough, this is basically chicken piccata but with veal. *Scallopini* refers to a thinly sliced cut of meat. Veal, being one of the most tender meats, melts in your mouth like butter.

6–8 small, thinly sliced veal cutlets, about 1 pound (450g)

1 pinch of flaky sea salt

Freshly ground black pepper

½ cup all-purpose flour

3 tablespoons unsalted butter

2 tablespoons extra virgin olive oil

½ cup white wine

2 tablespoons capers, drained

Juice of ½ lemon

¼ bunch of Italian flat-leaf parsley, leaves picked off and finely chopped

1 Pat the veal cutlets dry with a paper towel and lightly season with salt and pepper.

2 Place the all-purpose flour in a shallow bowl. Dredge each veal cutlet in flour, shaking off any excess. Set aside on a plate.

3 In a large skillet over medium heat, warm 2 tablespoons butter and the olive oil. When the fats are hot, add the veal and cook for 3 or 4 minutes per side, turning the pieces carefully with tongs to avoid spitting. Transfer the veal to a plate and set aside.

4 In the same skillet, warm the remaining 1 tablespoon butter. Add the white wine, capers, and lemon juice, and simmer for 2 minutes or until the wine reduces by half.

5 Return the veal to the pan, and gently turn to coat in the sauce.

6 Add the Italian flat-leaf parsley, and remove from the heat. Serve on top of a bed of insalata tricolore (page 200), drizzling any remaining sauce evenly over the top.

TIP *For thinner veal cutlets, arrange the veal between 2 sheets of plastic wrap on a cutting board. Use a meat pounder to evenly flatten the veal into ¼-inch (0.5cm) slices. The thinner the better, in my opinion.*

BUON APPETITO, BETCH!

COTOLETTA ALLA MILANESE
(BREADED VEAL CUTLET)

"co-tow-let-ah al-la me-lah-neh-seh"

SERVES: 4
PREP: 15 minutes
COOK: 30 minutes

Crisp and tender veal cutlet is a signature dish of Milan. Enjoy this breaded veal cutlet on a bed of fresh arugula salad dressed in olive oil and lemon, or in a sandwich.

6–8 cutlets veal loin, about 1 pound (450g)

2 eggs

1 pinch of flaky sea salt

Freshly ground black pepper

2 cups bread crumbs

4 tablespoons unsalted butter

1–2 cups light olive oil, for frying

SPECIAL EQUIPMENT

Meat pounder

1 On a cutting board lined with parchment paper, lay the veal loin cutlets with a little room to spread, and place another sheet of parchment on top. Using a meat pounder, gently and systematically tenderize and spread the cutlets to an even thickness of about ¼ inch (0.5cm) all over.

2 In a shallow bowl, beat the eggs with a little salt and pepper. In a second shallow bowl, add the bread crumbs.

3 Dip each cutlet into the egg to coat and then into bread crumbs to cover. Set aside the bread-crumbed cutlets on a plate.

4 In a large pan over medium-high heat, melt the butter into the olive oil. When the fats are hot (test their readiness by frying a bread crumb; if it immediately starts fizzing and popping, the fats are hot), add the cutlets in small batches and fry for 4 or 5 minutes per side or until golden and crispy. Transfer the cutlets to a paper towel–lined plate, dab with another paper towel to remove excess fat, and repeat with the remaining cutlets.

5 Serve hot and with a side of patate al forno (see page 209).

TIP *To make your own bread crumbs, tear some stale bread into small pieces and toast in a warm oven for 10 to 15 minutes or until evenly crisped. Crumble the pieces to consistent-sized small crumbs, and allow to cool before using. Store any extra bread crumbs in an airtight container in the fridge for up to 1 week.*

BUON APPETITO, BETCH!

OSSO BUCO MILANESE

"oh-so boo-ko me-lah-neh-seh"

SERVES: 4
PREP: 15 minutes
COOK: 2 hours 10 minutes

For years growing up, all I would order at my dad's restaurants was rigatoni alla buttera (see page 128). I never ordered any other dish...until the day I tasted osso buco. *Osso buco* translates to "bone with the hole" and is often served alongside risotto. You will be hooked on the tenderness and how effortlessly it melts in your mouth. My father taught me to suck out the marrow, which is the best part of the dish!

4 veal shanks, each 1 inch (2.5cm) thick

⅓ cup all-purpose flour

4 tablespoons unsalted butter

3 tablespoons extra virgin olive oil

1 medium yellow onion, diced into ½-inch (1.25cm) pieces

1 celery stalk, diced into ½-inch (1.25cm) cubes

1 carrot, diced into ½-inch (1.25cm) cubes

1 pinch of flaky sea salt

Freshly ground black pepper

½ cup dry white wine

2 cups vegetable or chicken broth, plus more as needed

1 tablespoon tomato paste

1 bay leaf

1 rosemary sprig

FOR THE GREMOLATA:

½ bunch of Italian flat-leaf parsley, leaves picked off and finely chopped

1 garlic clove, minced

Zest of ½ lemon

1–2 tablespoons extra virgin olive oil

1 Prepare the veal shanks by carefully cutting off the white connective tissue surrounding the shank using kitchen shears or a sharp knife.

2 Add the all-purpose flour to a shallow bowl or plate. Lightly coat each piece of veal in flour on both sides. Set aside.

3 In a large, deep frying pan over low heat, warm the butter and olive oil. When the fats are hot, make a soffritto by adding the yellow onion, celery, and carrot, and frying for 5 minutes or until soft.

4 Place the floured veal shanks in the pan with the soffritto. Increase the heat to medium, and cook for 5 minutes per side or until the meat has a little color on its edges. Season with a little salt and pepper.

5 Pour the white wine into the pan and let it simmer to reduce by about half.

6 In a small saucepan over medium heat, warm the vegetable broth. When it's hot, pour it into the pan with the shanks. Reduce the heat to medium-low and let it simmer.

7 Add the tomato paste, bay leaf, and rosemary, and stir gently to create a lovely sauce. Cover and cook on low for 1½ to 2 hours, turning the veal shanks carefully every 30 minutes or so to prevent them from sticking to the pan. Add a splash of broth, if needed. (As they cook, the meat will start to slide off the bone.)

8 Meanwhile, prepare the gremolata. In a small bowl, combine the Italian flat-leaf parsley, garlic, lemon zest, and olive oil.

9 A few minutes before the cooking time is up, add the gremolata to the frying pan and stir. Remove the bay leaf. Serve hot.

BUON APPETITO, BETCH!

BEEF BRACIOLE

"bra-choh-leh"

SERVES: 4
PREP: 20 minutes
COOK: 2½ hours

Another Sunday Funday dish, beef braciole takes a few hours to prepare, but one bite will leave you with a big ol' smile. Let's see if you can pronounce this one the right way: it's *bra-choh-leh*, not "brashzol." You'll get away with saying it wrong; everyone does.

4 pieces of flank steak, each about 4 ounces (115g)

1 pinch of flaky sea salt

Freshly ground black pepper

4–8 slices prosciutto

½ cup bread crumbs

¾ cup freshly grated provolone cheese

½ cup freshly grated Parmesan cheese

4 garlic cloves, minced

½ cup Italian flat-leaf parsley

6 tablespoons extra virgin olive oil

1 yellow onion, finely chopped

½ cup red wine

1 × 28-ounce (794g) can crushed San Marzano tomatoes

1 bay leaf

¼ cup chopped basil, for garnish

Freshly grated Parmesan cheese, for garnish (optional)

SPECIAL EQUIPMENT

Cocktail sticks or kitchen twine

1   Place each flank steak on a cutting board between 2 pieces of parchment paper and pound with a meat pounder or rolling pin until it's about ¼ inch (0.5cm) thick. Aim for a shape that's about 6 inches (15cm) long and 3 inches (7.5cm) wide. Season with salt and pepper, set on a large plate, and repeat with the remaining steaks.

2   Place 1 or 2 slices of prosciutto on top of each piece of pounded flank steak. Use your hands to gently push to adhere the prosciutto to the steak.

3   In a medium bowl, mix the bread crumbs, provolone cheese, shredded Parmesan cheese, ½ of the garlic, and the parsley. Add 2 tablespoons of olive oil and mix to combine.

4   Spread 1 or 2 tablespoons of the bread crumb mixture evenly on top of the prosciutto slices, and press down. Then, starting at the shorter side, firmly roll and tuck the steak into a cylinder, wrapping the bread crumb mixture inside. Use a cocktail stick like a sewing needle to secure the edges of the steak. Alternatively, you can tie a piece of uncolored kitchen twine around the middle to secure it. Repeat with the remaining pieces of steak.

5   In a Dutch oven or a large, deep frying pan set over medium-high heat, warm 2 tablespoons olive oil. When the oil is hot, add the bracioles and evenly sear for 4 to 6 minutes or until the outside has a good amount of color. Remove from the pan and set aside.

6   In the same pot, add the remaining 2 tablespoons of olive oil. Add the remaining garlic and the onion and sauté for a few minutes or until lightly golden.

7   Add the red wine,and simmer for 1 or 2 minutes or until the wine has reduced by half.

8   In a medium bowl, further crush the San Marzano tomatoes with your hands or break them into small pieces with a spoon and then add them to the pot. Season with salt and pepper and add the bay leaf. Reduce the heat to medium-low.

9   Return the bracioles to the pot. Bring to a simmer and then reduce the heat to low. Cover and cook for 2 hours, checking every 30 minutes, and turning the bracioles if necessary. You may need to add a splash more water to avoid the sauce getting too thick.

10 Remove the bay leaf. Transfer the braciole to serving plates. Cover with a generous amount of the sauce, garnish with basil and grated Parmesan (if using), and serve with cooked pasta.

BUON APPETITO, BETCH!

SALSICCIA E FRIARIELLI
(SAUSAGE AND BROCCOLI RABE)

"sal-sea-cha eh free-are-ee-yell-ee"

SERVES: 4
PREP: 15 minutes
COOK: 30 minutes

Sausage and broccoli rabe are best friends in Neapolitan cuisine. On pizza, pasta, bread, or simply just as is, I can't get enough of these two. In Naples, the bitter green broccoli rabe is known as *friarielli*. Others may know it as rapini. Whatever the name, it's the Italian broccoli but with much more of a kick.

3 small bunches of broccoli rabe, about 21 ounces (600g)

4 links spicy Italian sausage, about 12 ounces (340g)

½ glass dry white wine

2 tablespoons extra virgin olive oil

2 garlic cloves, minced

1 teaspoon red pepper flakes

1 pinch of flaky sea salt

1   Rinse the broccoli rabe well under cold water, and shake to dry. Trim off 1 or 2 inches from the base of the stem and discard.

2   Bring a large pot of water to a rolling boil over high heat. Add the broccoli rabe and blanch for 2 or 3 minutes or until bright green and crisp-tender. (Blanching takes away the bitterness.) Drain and set aside.

3   In a medium frying pan over medium-high heat, add the sausages with just enough water to cover the bottom of the pan and steam for 10 minutes. Pierce the sausages with a fork and pour off the water and any fat that drains out of the sausages.

4   Add the white wine to the pan, reduce the heat to medium, and simmer for about 10 minutes or until the sausages are cooked through and well browned.

5   In a separate medium frying pan over medium-low eat, warm the extra virgin olive oil. When the oil is hot, add the garlic and red pepper flakes and fry until golden.

6   Add the blanched broccoli rabe, season with salt, and cook, using tongs to move things around, for 2 minutes.

7   Add the browned sausages to the pan with the broccoli rabe and drizzle some olive oil over the top. Serve hot.

BUON APPETITO, BETCH!

AGNELLO ALLA SCOTTADITO
(ROMAN LAMB CHOPS)

"ah-gneh-low ah-la scoh-tah-dito"

SERVES: 4
PREP: 10 minutes (plus 1 hour to marinate)
COOK: 10 minutes

Agnello alla scottadito (pronounced *ahn-yellow ah-la sko-to-deeto*) is the Roman name for grilled lamb chops, and *scottadito* translates as "finger burning." If your fingers don't burn, then you're not doing it right. This dish is served hot from the grill and right into your hands to be eaten. Rosemary goes beautifully with lamb dishes and the chops taste great served with patate al forno (page 209).

4 lamb chops, each 5–7 ounces (140–200g)
3 garlic cloves, minced
4 tablespoons finely chopped rosemary leaves
4–5 tablespoons extra virgin olive oil
1 pinch of flaky sea salt
Freshly ground black pepper

1. Unwrap the lamb chops and place them on a tray or medium plate.

2. In a small bowl, combine the garlic, rosemary, extra virgin olive oil, salt, and pepper.

3. Using your hands or a pastry brush, thoroughly coat the lamb in the herb mixture. Cover with plastic wrap and refrigerate for at least 1 hour or overnight.

4. Preheat a grill, barbecue, or a ridged skillet pan to high.

5. Throw the chops on the grill and cook, keeping the heat high, until well browned on the outside. About 2 to 4 minutes per side will cook them medium. Serve immediately.

BUON APPETITO, BETCH!

CONTORNI

INSALATA TRICOLORE
(THREE COLOR SALAD)

"een-sah-lah-tah tree-coh-lore-eh"

SERVES: 4
PREP: 15 minutes
COOK: None

A salad with the colors of the Italian flag? Now that's my type of salad. In this flavorful side salad, you get the green from the arugula, the white from the endives, and the red from the cabbage. This one is fresh like the Prince of Bel Air.

FOR THE DRESSING:
2 tablespoons fresh lemon juice
2 teaspoons Dijon mustard
1 garlic clove, puréed
⅓ cup extra virgin olive oil
1 pinch of flaky sea salt
Freshly ground black pepper

FOR THE SALAD:
3 cups arugula, about 3 ounces (85g)
½ head radicchio, or 2 handfuls of red baby salad leaves
2 heads of endive, ends trimmed and cut into slices crosswise
1 handful of freshly shaved Parmesan cheese
1 pinch of flaky sea salt
Freshly ground black pepper

1   In a small bowl, whisk together the lemon juice, Dijon mustard, garlic, extra virgin olive oil, salt, and pepper.

2   In a large salad bowl, toss the arugula, radicchio, and endive. Add the dressing and toss to coat evenly.

3   Top with freshly shaved Parmesan cheese, salt, and pepper to taste, and serve.

TIP *To clean and cut the radicchio, start by removing any outer leaves that are wilted. Cut the radicchio in half, and remove the core. Slice the leaves finely across the middle.*

BUON APPETITO, BETCH!

PEPERONATA
(SWEET BELL PEPPERS)

"peh-per-on-ah-tah"

SERVES: 4
PREP: 10 minutes
COOK: 40 minutes

You will find this side dish at any gathering in Southern Italy. Sweet bell peppers and onions are cooked in a generous amount of olive oil—you can probably taste it as you're reading this, can't you? Either way, make it, betch!

- 4 tablespoons extra virgin olive oil
- 1 small yellow onion, sliced finely into half moons
- 2 garlic cloves, crushed with the side of a knife
- 4 red or yellow bell peppers, de-stemmed, de-seeded, and sliced lengthwise
- ¼ small bunch of basil, leaves picked off and roughly torn
- 1 pinch of flaky sea salt

1 In a large pan over medium-high heat, warm 3 tablespoons extra virgin olive oil. Add the yellow onion, reduce the heat to medium, and sauté for about 5 to 8 minutes or until the onion softens.

2 Add the garlic and sauté for 1 minute.

3 Add the sliced bell peppers and mix well. Reduce the heat to medium-low, cover, and cook, stirring occasionally to ensure the peppers don't stick or burn, for 20 to 30 minutes or until the peppers are very soft.

4 Garnish with basil, a pinch of salt, and a drizzle of the remaining olive oil, and serve.

BUON APPETITO, BETCH!

SPINACI RIPASSATI IN PADELLA
(SAUTÉED SPINACH)

"spin-ah-chee ree-pah-sah-tee een pah-del-a"

SERVES: 4
PREP: 5 minutes
COOK: 5 minutes

Mama always told me to eat my spinach. Listen to mama and you'll have muscles you had no idea existed. This simple sauteed spinach is the best way to do it, keeping it simple, clean, and delish. Eat those greens, BETCH. EAT THOSE GREENS!

1½ pounds (680g) fresh baby spinach

3 tablespoons extra virgin olive oil

4 garlic cloves, peeled and very finely sliced

Flaky sea salt

¼ teaspoon red pepper flakes (optional)

1 pinch of freshly ground black pepper

Lemon wedges, for serving

1 Fill a large bowl with cold water and add the spinach to clean. Dry completely with a salad spinner or kitchen towel and trim off any long or woody stalks.

2 In a large pan over medium heat, warm the extra virgin olive oil. When the oil is hot, add the garlic and sauté for 1 minute or until fragrant. Do not allow it to brown or burn.

3 Add the spinach, salt, red pepper flakes (if using), and pepper, and mix well. I find using tongs helps. Cook for 2 minutes or until the spinach has wilted. Mix again and cook gently for 2 minutes more or until the spinach is soft.

4 Drizzle with some freshly squeezed lemon juice and serve.

BUON APPETITO, BETCH!

PISELLI ALLA FIORENTINA
(FLORETINE-STYLE SPRING PEAS)

"pee-sell-ee ah-la floor-en-tina"

SERVES: 4
PREP: 5 minutes
COOK: 18 minutes

The saltiness from the pancetta combined with the sweetness from the peas makes this dish unique. This side dish is typically served with meat but my family enjoys it the most as a pasta dish.. yes I ate a lot of pasta growing up!!

3 tablespoons extra virgin olive oil

2 garlic cloves, peeled and sliced

3 ounces (85g) pancetta, diced

1 pound (450g) fresh or frozen small garden peas, about 2 pounds (1kg) with shells

1 teaspoon sugar

1 pinch of flaky sea salt

Freshly ground black pepper

1 tablespoon chopped Italian flat-leaf parsley, for garnish

1   In a large pot or Dutch oven over medium-high heat, warm the extra virgin olive oil. Add the garlic and pancetta and fry for 2 to 3 minutes or until the garlic is golden and the pancetta is crisp.

2   Reduce the heat to medium. Add the peas, sugar, 1 cup water, salt, and pepper. Cover and simmer for 15 minutes, removing the lid for the last few minutes if there is still some liquid to evaporate.

3   Remove from the heat, garnish with Italian flat-leaf parsley, and serve.

TIP *Fresh spring peas are in season during the summer months if you want to level up this recipe.*

BUON APPETITO, BETCH!

PATATE AL FORNO
(OVEN-ROASTED POTATOES)

"pah-tah-teh al four-no"

SERVES: 4–6
PREP: 20 minutes
COOK: 45 minutes

Potatoes are like pasta—they can go with everything and they're easy to make. I added rosemary to this recipe because that's what my mamma did for us growing up. Pair this side dish with Chicken Scarpariello (page 176). Trust me!

2 pounds (1kg) small or medium Yukon Gold potatoes

5 tablespoons extra virgin olive oil

Flaky sea salt and freshly crushed black pepper

1–2 rosemary sprigs

2 garlic cloves

1   Preheat the oven to 400°F (200°C).

2   Wash the Yukon Gold potatoes and remove any eyes, cuts, or bruises with a small, sharp knife. Cut the potatoes into pieces about 1 inch (2.5cm) across—a large bite size.

3   Bring a large pot of salted water to a boil over high heat. Add the potatoes and cook for 5 minutes. Drain the potatoes and arrange in a single layer on a baking sheet.

4   Drizzle the potatoes with extra virgin olive oil and season generously with salt, pepper, and the rosemary.

5   Lightly crush the garlic with the heel of your hand or the side of a knife and add to the baking pan.

6   Bake for 30 to 40 minutes, shaking the pan every 10 minutes to prevent the potatoes from sticking, until the potatoes are golden and soft in the middle.

7   Serve warm.

BUON APPETITO, BETCH!

INDEX

A

B

C

D–E

I

Impepata Di Cozze (Peppered Steamed Mussels), 62

Imperia pasta machine, 74

ingredients, essential, 24–25

Insalata Di Fagioli (Tuscan Bean Salad), 34

Insalata Tricolore (Tricolor Salad), 200

Ischian Rabbit Stew (Coniglio All'Ischitana), 180

Italian bread/baguette
Bruschetta, 45
Caponata with Crostini, 46
Panzanella Con Burrata (Burrata Panzanella Salad), 42
Spaghetti and Meatballs, 143–144

Italian sausage
Chicken Scarpariello, 176
Orecchiette con Salsiccia e Cime di Rapa (Orecchiette with Sausage and Broccoli Rabe), 135
Salsiccia e Friarielli (Sausage and Broccoli Rabe), 192

K–L

Kalamata olives
Pesce All'acqua Pazza (Fish in Crazy Water), 167
Puttanesca, 107
Salmone Alla Siciliana (Sicilian-Style Salmon), 163

lamb chops, in Agnello Alla Scottadito (Roman Lamb Chops), 195

lasagna
Homemade Fresh Pasta, 72–73
Lasagna Bolognese, 136–139

lemon(s)
Beef Carpaccio, 37
Carciofi Alla Roman (Roman Braised Artichokes), 50
Gamberoni Alla Griglia (Grilled Shrimp), 155
Penne con Salmone Ricotta e Limone (Penne with Salmon, Ricotta, and Lemon), 112
Roasted Branzino, 160
Shrimp Scampi, 156

lentils, in Tubetti e Lenticchie (Pasta and Lentils), 90

linguine
Aglio Olio Peperoncino (Spaghetti with Garlic and Olive Oil), 78
Homemade Fresh Pasta, 72–73
Linguine alla Vongole (Linguine with Clams), 108

Lobster Ravioli, 116–119

M

machine, making fresh pasta by, 74

Manicotti, 102–105

marinara sauce
Homemade Marinara Sauce, 153
Manicotti, 102–105
Spaghetti Marinara, 82

Marinated Anchovies (Alici Marinate), 33

melon, in Prosciutto e Melone (Prosciutto and Melon), 30

mint leaves
Carciofi Alla Roman (Roman Braised Artichokes), 50
Prosciutto e Melone (Prosciutto and Melon), 30

mixer, making pasta dough with a, 74

mozzarella cheese, in Manicotti, 102–105. *See also* fresh mozzarella

mushrooms
Chicken Marsala, 175
Risotto Alla Mare e Monti (Mountains and Sea Risotto), 171

mussels
Cioppino, 168
Impepata Di Cozze (Peppered Steamed Mussels), 62

N

Neapolitan-Style Italian Meat Sauce (Rigatoni Alla Ragù Napoletano), 131

O

onions
Baccalà Alla Livornese (Salted Cod), 164
Beef Braciole, 191
Caponata with Crostini, 46
Chicken Scarpariello, 176
Insalata Di Fagioli, 34
Lasagna Bolognese, 136–139
Manicotti, 102
Osso Buco Milanese, 188
Panzanella Con Burrata (Burrata Panzanella Salad), 42